National Assessment and the Teaching of English

NCTE Committee to Study the National Assessment of Educational Progress

John C. Mellon, University of Illinois at Chicago Circle, Chair
Ruth K. J. Cline, University of Colorado
Donald R. Gallo, Central Connecticut State College
Doris V. Gunderson, U.S. Department of Health, Education, and Welfare
Richard Lloyd-Jones, University of Iowa
Donald Seybold, Purdue University
Robert E. Shafer, Arizona State University
L. Ramon Veal, University of Georgia
Gladys Veidemanis, North High School, Oshkosh, Wisconsin

Consultant Readers

Rose Duarte, McClintock High School, Tempe, Arizona
Mattie H. Eley, Atlanta Public Schools, Atlanta, Georgia
Robert S. Fay, Contoocook Valley Regional High School, Peterborough, New Hampshire
Rose M. Feinberg, Lowell State College, Lowell, Massachusetts
Helen P. Gillotte, J. M. Harlan High School, Chicago, Illinois
La Ruth Hackney Gray, City School District, New Rochelle, New York
Donna Haglin, Southern Hills Junior High School, Boulder, Colorado
Dorothy M. Nutting, Hoover Elementary School, Mason City, Iowa
Daniel C. Ward, Cedar Shoals High School, Athens, Georgia
Anne Knight Watson, Cabarrus County Schools, Concord, North Carolina

National Assessment and the Teaching of English

Results of the First National Assessment of Educational Progress in Writing, Reading, and Literature—Implications for Teaching and Measurement in the English Language Arts

John C. Mellon
University of Illinois at Chicago Circle

National Council of Teachers of English
1111 Kenyon Road, Urbana, Illinois, 61801

Acknowledgments

"Poem" (As the Cat) by William Carlos Williams is from *Collected Earlier Poems.* Copyright 1938 by New Directions Publishing Corporation. Reprinted by permission of New Directions Publishing Corporation.

"Sport" by W. H. Davies is from *The Complete Poems of W. H. Davies.* Copyright © 1963 by Jonathan Cape Ltd. Reprinted by permission of Wesleyan University Press, Jonathan Cape Ltd., and Mrs. H. M. Davies.

"Into My Heart an Air That Kills" by A. E. Housman is from "A Shropshire Lad"—Authorised Edition—from *The Collected Poems of A. E. Housman.* Copyright 1939, 1940, © 1965 by Holt, Rinehart and Winston, Inc. Copyright © 1967, 1968 by Robert E. Symons. Reprinted by permission of Holt, Rinehart and Winston, Publishers, and by The Society of Authors as the literary representative of the Estate of A. E. Housman, and Jonathan Cape Ltd., publishers of A. E. Housman's *Collected Poems.*

NCTE Editorial Board

Charles R. Cooper, Evelyn M. Copeland, Bernice E. Cullinan, Richard Lloyd-Jones, Frank Zidonis, Robert F. Hogan, *ex officio,* Paul O'Dea, *ex officio.*

Book Design: Rob Carter
NCTE Stock Number 32235
Copyright © 1975 by the National Council of Teachers of English.
All rights reserved. Printed in the United States of America.

Library of Congress Cataloging in Publication Data

Mellon, John C
　National assessment and the teaching of English.

　　1. Language arts.   2.   English language—Examinations.
3.   National Assessment of Educational Progress (Project).
I. Title.
LB1576.M44   420'.76   75-28674
ISBN 0-8141-3223-5

Contents

Chapter One: Introduction — 1

What This Report Contains   2
How This Report Was Written   2
Who Should Read This Report   3
Why This Report Is Important   4

Chapter Two: Facts about National Assessment — 6

Chapter Three: The Writing Assessment — 14

The Writing Objectives   14
The Writing Exercises   15
Acceptable/Unacceptable Exercises   16
Yes/No Exercises   19
Essay Exercises   21
Holistic Scoring of Essay Responses   22
Results of the Essay Exercises   23
The Uses of Holistic Scoring   27
The 13–17 Overall-Quality Comparison   28
The Study of Writing Mechanics   29
Mechanics in Perspective   32
Assessing Writing and Teaching Writing   33
Formulating Composition Topics   34
Summary   37

Chapter Four: The Reading Assessment — 39

The Reading Objectives   40
The Reading Themes   41
The Reading Exercises   42

Answering Multiple-Choice Exercises   42
Presentation of the Results   44
Literal-Comprehension Sentences   45
Inference Sentences   59
The Rate and Comprehension Assessment   67
Problems in Analyzing Reading Comprehension   68
Observations on Comprehension Difficulty   69
A Warning about the Reading Themes   70
Judging the Reading Results   70
National Assessment and Grade-Level Scores   72

Chapter Five: The Literature Assessment 75

The Literature Objectives and Exercises   76
Knowledge of Literary Works   77
Understanding Literary Language   77
Assessment Questions versus Teaching Questions   82
Assessing Response to Literature   84
Multiple-Choice-plus-Reasons Response Exercises   86
Channeling-Questions-plus-Oral-Answers Response Exercises   88
Written-Essay Response Exercises   89
Survey of Reading Habits and Attitudes   91
Interpreting the Literature Assessment   96
Selecting the Content of a Literature Assessment   97

Chapter Six: Summary Discussion 100

Our Students' Knowledge of English   100
Revised Objectives for the Second-Round Assessments   102
Positive Aspects of National Assessment   107
Problem Areas: Motivational Level and Usefulness of the
    Data Collected   108
Problem Areas: Comprehensiveness of the Assessments   109
A Warning against the Local Use of NAEP Exercises   110
Limitations of Statewide Use of NAEP Exercises   110
Local Accountability Measurement Using NAEP Procedures   111
Advantages of NAEP-Style Accountability Measurement   114
Final Thoughts on Measuring Teaching and Learning   115

Appendix A: Reading Passages 119

Appendix B: Literary Works 125

Chapter One

Introduction

The National Assessment of Educational Progress (NAEP) is a federally funded survey of the educational attainments of representative samples of American young people and adults at four age levels. Beginning in 1964, planners for National Assessment targeted ten subject areas to be assessed regularly every four years. Three of these subjects form the core of the language arts and English curriculum—writing, reading, and literature. Assessments were begun in 1969, and the first in a series of official NAEP reports on the initial writing assessment appeared late in 1970. Reports on the reading and literature assessments reached print in 1972 and 1973 respectively and continue to be released up to this writing.

In the early years, some educators feared that National Assessment would sooner or later become a nationwide achievement test and might lead to the establishment of a national curriculum including the mandatory measurement of accountability. But these fears have proven groundless. In fact, NAEP was designed specifically to measure the state of knowledge of various academic subjects without the need for administering batteries of achievement tests to the student population at large. Furthermore, NAEP has maintained such a low profile within the education profession, and its results have so infrequently lent themselves to journalistic sensationalism, that the majority of teachers are barely aware of its existence. Consequently, we are in danger of missing an opportunity to gain from its findings a great deal of practical information about teaching and measurement in the English areas.

The following booklet aims to remedy this situation. It summarizes in detail the findings of the initial writing, reading, and literature assessments and interprets this factual data from a number of perspectives. It is intended for English language arts teachers at every level, as well as curriculum and research specialists, and for all other persons concerned about teaching and learning in English.

What This Report Contains

More specifically, this booklet provides factual information and interpretive statements of two kinds. One kind of factual information describes what National Assessment is and how it works. The other kind presents the actual contents of the writing, reading, and literature assessments, synopsizing the questions asked and the answers obtained. Although presented as numerical percentages in tabular format, the latter are discussed in simple language entirely free of the technical vocabulary of the statistician or measurement specialist.

The interpretive portions of this booklet dwell equally upon the nature of National Assessment exercises and the results they yielded. Basically two types of interpretation are given. One type, pertaining to classroom teaching, deals with the learnings that students of different ages may be expected to achieve, and stresses, perhaps surprisingly, the importance of valid assessment activities in ongoing teaching just as much as in testing. The other type consists of suggestions and warnings about the use of National Assessment exercises at the local level, in individual classrooms or buildings, or on a district-wide or statewide basis.

How This Report Was Written

At its 1973 annual convention, as a result of resolutions adopted there and at previous conventions, the National Council of Teachers of English established a committee to study the National Assessment of Educational Progress and named the author of this booklet as committee chair. Shortly thereafter, in response to a proposal submitted by the present author, the Utilization/Applications Department of National Assessment granted funds to NCTE to support the preparation of this interpretive report. As with all National Council publications, the NCTE Editorial Board exercised approval rights over publication of the manuscript. The Council also bears the cost of manufacturing and distributing the report and holds copyright to its text.

In writing this booklet, the author with NCTE approval agreed not to critique the procedures used by NAEP in developing objectives and exercises in each subject area or in selecting samples of respondents at the different age levels. In return, the author enjoyed full freedom to interpret the curricular implications of National Assessment results as he saw fit and to discuss both the form and the content of NAEP exercises as well as the results they yielded. This last point is a matter of some importance, for truly, in educational measurement as in any other, the measuring gauge and its readings are mutually dependent and inseparable.

Credit for a great many of the observations and conclusions presented in this booklet goes to individual members of the NCTE Committee to Study the National Assessment, to the ten consultant readers also named in the front pages, to John C. Maxwell, deputy executive secretary of NCTE, and to Rexford G. Brown of NAEP's Utilization/ Applications Department. All these persons contributed invaluable suggestions about what needed saying and how best to say it. To each, the readers of this report together with its author owe a substantial debt of gratitude.

Obviously, however, there was not total agreement on all that appears herein, nor could there ever be, one supposes, when the points at issue are matters of interpretation rather than cold fact, and when they pertain to such an emotionally charged topic as the content of a nationwide English assessment. Rather than avoid potentially controversial observations, which ultimately would have meant omitting interpretations of any kind, the author of this report assumed responsibility for determining its content and included material with which some readers may disagree. The goal throughout was to provoke fruitful thought about the appropriate uses of assessment in both teaching and testing. Wherever possible, interpretive conclusions are accompanied by the reasons which prompted them. It is hoped that readers will weigh and evaluate the merits of these reasons, and they are free to accept or reject the interpretive commentary as they see fit.

Who Should Read This Report

This booklet is intended for a broad audience of professional and lay persons united by the commitment to offer young people the best English education that human resources and talents can provide. Prospective readers include many groups—heads of English departments, academic coordinators, directors of English and the language arts, building administrators, and school superintendents; parents, persons in civic and parental organizations, and members of school boards; educational researchers and consultants, popular education writers, and college professors of English and education.

But the principal audience, those to whom this report hopes to be most useful, are classroom teachers of the language arts and English. The most important person in English education remains as always the frontline teacher, whose daily business is direct interaction with students. Upon the teacher's shoulders alone rests the ultimate responsibility for developing in students the abilities, skills, attitudes, and values comprising the language arts, as well as for presenting the subject matter of English. It is the classroom teacher who will benefit most from the lessons National Assessment can teach us about teaching.

Because a wide readership is intended, and because preferences differ even among persons in identical professional roles, readers may find that the following report includes either more or less of certain material than they would otherwise desire, or that it goes into topics too deeply or not deeply enough. Unfortunately, where one man's meat is another's poison, happy mediums are impossible to attain. Since it is easier to skip over what is written than to read what is omitted, it seemed preferable to err on the side of including too much rather than too little.

Readers are therefore encouraged to read selectively, and numerous subheads are provided to guide the process. Some persons may wish information not contained in the report (adult scores, for example, or details on the performance of subgroups), and for this they must turn to the original NAEP documents. Naturally this booklet does not presume to say the last word on the curricular implications of National Assessment or on the optimal means of measuring learnings in English. Part of its very purpose is to stimulate readers to formulate such conclusions on their own.

Why This Report Is Important

The National Assessment of Educational Progress, whose funding level ranges from four to six million dollars annually, is America's largest continuing project devoted to the systematic gathering of factual data on the school-sponsored learnings of young people. For many, this point alone would justify the preparation of an informational booklet such as the following. But there are other reasons as well.

First, it is important that educational practitioners have available a single concise summation of National Assessment findings in the three English areas. No such summation currently exists. Reviews of the English Assessments have appeared separately in professional journals, but these are scattered in location and selective in their treatment of NAEP findings. Moreover, reading the original National Assessment reports is a difficult task that virtually all teachers have understandably avoided. Yet there are many things we can learn from these findings, and much we should know if we are to prevent their misuse.

Second, factual results of any broadly based assessment should be accompanied by a full-scale professional interpretation, for numerical data by itself is meaningless. NAEP, however, in keeping with its censuslike mission, has largely discouraged the writers of its official reports from engaging in interpretation, believing that this function should be left to scholars and teachers, popular education writers, or anyone else in the public who cares to undertake it. Thus it is important that English teachers have access to an interpretation of NAEP findings that is informed, comprehensive, responsible, and as near to objective as possible.

Introduction 5

Third, it is crucial that professionals and lay persons alike recognize that National Assessment is different from typical achievement testing programs, whose purpose is to determine how well individual teachers have taught and individual learners learned. NAEP's aim is rather to tell what students in general know and can do. From this information, properly interpreted, teachers can learn a great deal that will further improve their teaching. This is a refrain re-echoed throughout the following report.

Fourth, it is important to remember that second-round assessments are now being conducted in each subject area, thus permitting comparisons to be made between findings of the first assessments and those of the second. Almost certainly there will be downtrends as well as uptrends in second-round results, and the lower scores will surely receive much attention from educational critics and the media. A thorough knowledge of National Assessment methodology will be invaluable in allaying anxieties and preventing unwarranted sensationalist furor, whether the second-round scores are up or down.

Fifth, it is imperative that National Assessment exercises, if they are to be employed in any manner at the local level, be adapted in ways that will ensure their valid use. Unmodified, however, they are wholly unsuited for establishing accountability, for measuring and evaluating the competence of teachers, or for comparing the standing of one school district with that of another. Yet it is increasingly apparent in present times that local school officials are setting the stage for just such misuses by calling for the utilization of National Assessment exercises to obtain the test information they feel necessary for deciding questions of local educational finance.

In the end, the most significant understandings to be derived from this report extend beyond any of the foregoing points and embrace instead the broader topics of educational measurement, evaluation, assessment, testing and accountability. No other concerns over the past half decade have produced more frustration, intimidation, and outbursts of irrationality within the English teaching profession. Yet it is pointless to rail at the mere fact of testing. Test exercises by themselves merit scant attention. The important questions are who decides to use them with which students for what purposes, and what is said and what is believed about the results. The following booklet applies these questions specifically to the National Assessments of writing, reading, and literature. But it attempts to discuss them in ways that are applicable to testing and the evaluation of learning and teaching in general, at every educational level.

Chapter Two

Facts about National Assessment

The National Assessment of Educational Progress observed its tenth birthday in 1974, but very few English teachers celebrated the occasion, if indeed they even knew what National Assessment was. For example, in a poll of twenty experienced teachers in the author's graduate seminar in English education, conducted just prior to this writing, only five of the twenty had so much as heard of NAEP. Four of the five were unable to provide even a single item of information about Assessment findings, and the fifth thought that National Assessment was a proposal to levy a nationwide education tax. The following questions and answers thus attempt to provide a concise factual guide to National Assessment, its purposes and procedures.

What is the National Assessment of Educational Progress?

It is a nationwide censuslike survey of the educational attainments of representative samples of American youth aged nine, thirteen, and seventeen, and adults in the 26–35 age bracket. In general, though not in all cases, these turn out to be students in grades four, eight, and twelve, plus adults averaging ten years beyond school.

How was NAEP begun?

In 1964, following discussions between the United States Commissioner of Education Francis Keppel and President John Gardner of the Carnegie Corporation, Dr. Ralph Tyler of the Center for Advanced Study in the Behavioral Sciences at Stanford University was asked to chair a distinguished group of Americans joined together as the Exploratory Committee on Assessing the Progress of Education. Planning for the project consumed five years. In 1969 its governance was shifted to the Education Commission of the States. The project title became National Assessment of Educational Progress, and the first assessments were conducted in the schools.

What are the purposes of National Assessment?

One purpose is to measure any growth or decline of educational attainment from one assessment time to another. Another purpose is to provide comprehensive information about the knowledge, abilities, and attitudes of young people in any subject at any given time—information useful in a variety of ways to professional educators as well as concerned laymen, legislators, and philanthropic organizations.

Apart from its usefulness to teachers, why was this information considered important?

Federal support of education had reached an all-time high in the early sixties. NAEP proponents saw the question of accountability looming on the horizon. They argued that National Assessment's nonnormative sampling approach would be far less costly and generally more desirable than a universal nationwide achievement-testing program and that it would provide members of Congress with the information needed to make intelligent decisions about educational funding. Today, similar discussions are occurring the country over at the local level—a matter dealt with at length later in this booklet.

Who pays for NAEP?

National Assessment is financed primarily by the National Center for Education Statistics, Office of the Assistant Secretary for Education, Department of Health, Education, and Welfare. NAEP's parent body is the Education Commission of the States, an organization supported in part by the Ford Foundation Fund for the Advancement of Education and led by a membership of state governors, chief state school officers, legislators, and lay people.

What subjects are assessed, and how often?

Ten subjects are covered: reading, writing, literature, science, mathematics, citizenship, music, social studies, art, and career and occupational development. Each subject was originally to be assessed every four years, but this interval has been increased in some cases. As of this writing, no second-cycle results have been reported in the English areas, although reading and writing have been reassessed, and literature will be reassessed in four years.

How does National Assessment work?

NAEP utilizes the same principle of sampling statistics employed in public opinion polling, namely, that the results obtained from a small but appropriately selected sample of respondents will be identical to those that would be obtained from the entire population which the sample represents.

How large are the samples of NAEP respondents?

Each exercise item in any assessment is answered by 2000 to 2500 respondents. Statisticians consider this number sufficiently large to allow precise statements to be inferred from the sample group and applied to the national population at any given age. No person is asked to devote more than 50 minutes, the general equivalent of one class period in school, to answering assessment items. Therefore, since a complete assessment in a given subject at a given age level consists of many hours of exercise time, from twenty-five to thirty thousand young people will be involved in any one assessment at any one age level.

How are the samples constructed?

Each group of 2000 to 2500 respondents is compiled in such a way that its membership proportionately represents the entire nation at the age level in question, described in terms of the following subgroups: geographical region (national quadrants); sex; color (nonblack and black); parents' highest educational level (four categories); size and type of community (seven categories).

How are the exercise items developed?

First, lists of learning objectives reflecting current school practice in each subject are formulated by scholars in the subject-matter field, school personnel, and groups of interested lay people. Then contracts are let to educational measurement companies for the development of exercise items measuring the extent to which these objectives are being attained. Prior to their use, all exercises must be approved by panels of scholars, teachers, and representatives of lay organizations. Exercises are field-tested ahead of time and rated as to difficulty level, and a mix of easy and difficult items is obtained. A limited number of exercises are developed from the outset by NAEP personnel, who have final say on the wording and content of all exercises used.

How are the exercises administered?

Exercise items are administered by persons in the employ of the measurement companies under contract to NAEP. For students in the lower three age brackets who are attending school, school buildings are selected in each of the four geographical regions, and students are identified therein in such a way that the sampling requirements for each age level are satisfied. These students meet with the NAEP examiner either individually or in small groups, according to the type of exercises to be administered. They are informed about the nature of the project in which they are participating and are told that their individual performances will not be reported to their teachers or parents or to anyone else and will in no way influence their academic records. The students are put at ease, urged to do their best, tested, and warmly thanked. Adult subjects and seventeen year olds not in school are treated in the same fashion, except that they are tested individually in their homes by appointment.

How are National Assessment results reported?

Basically, exercise items are treated one at a time. For items having correct and incorrect multiple answers, the number of persons who identify the correct answer is reported as a percentage of the total number who responded to the item. Thus, for example, if a national sample of 2000 thirteen year olds are asked a certain question and 1500 answer it correctly, NAEP would report a 75 percent correctness level for that item. This number is termed the "national percentage." For some reason, perhaps because we are accustomed to dealing with averages, many people refer to this figure as the "national average," but this is incorrect. The number is not an average of anything. It is simply the percentage of the total respondents to an item who answered it correctly. Correctness percentages are also reported for each subgroup in the total sample at every age level. Attitudinal exercises are scored and reported in the same way, except that the answers are not matters of correctness or incorrectness. Responses in the form of written compositions, required in the writing and literature assessments, are scored by an entirely different method which is fully described later in this booklet.

Are the assessments fully comprehensive in the several subject areas?

No claim for comprehensiveness is advanced by NAEP. Just as the respondents are a sample of the national population, so too are the exercises a sample of the total knowledge comprising each subject area. The difference is that the sample of people is known mathematically to be representative of the total population, whereas it is a matter of subjective judgment and no mathematics at all whether the exercises comprehensively represent the full body of subject matter to which they belong. As is discussed later in this booklet, the issue of comprehensiveness of NAEP exercises and their relationship to local teaching objectives is centrally important in determining the wisdom of using these exercises for local accountability testing.

Are all exercises used in any assessment released for public inspection?

No. Only half the exercises given in any one assessment are released. The other half are withheld so that they may be validly readministered during the next assessment cycle in that subject area, thus providing a comparison across time of knowledge of identical exercise content. The exercises presented in this report therefore constitute only about half of those actually included in the first reading, writing, and literature assessments.

Isn't National Assessment really a nationwide testing program?

Yes and no. Yes, only in the sense that assessment exercises measuring knowledge and abilities are cast in the usual format of test items—multiple choice and open-ended questions, essays in response to set topics, and so forth. But no, in that the samples of respondents are drawn in such a way that statements about the results cannot be applied to individual schools, school districts, or states. And no, in that a respondent's individual performance is never revealed, nor in fact does any one person participate in more than one-fourth of the full assessment in any subject.

What are the pass/fail norms for the assessments?

There are no pass/fail norms for any of the assessments, precisely because NAEP is not a test in the sense of an instrument designed to rank persons by achievement, or to sort them into categories of "passing" and "failure." In other words, the total performance of individual respondents is not summed up and rank-ordered in percentile or standard-score fashion, as is the case in standardized achievement tests and ordinary classroom testing.

Exactly what is the difference between a test and an assessment?

This is important. A test asks how many items of knowledge an individual possesses compared to other individuals within a group, and ordinarily rank-orders the individuals accordingly. An assessment, on the other hand, asks how many individuals in a group possess a certain item of knowledge. In an assessment it is only the items of knowledge that are rank-ordered, according to the number of individuals in the group who possess each one, reported as a percentage of the total who were asked the item. In short, a test, as the term is commonly used, tells how much an individual person knows about a body of knowledge in general, whereas an assessment, as defined by NAEP, indicates the extent to which individual items of knowledge are known by persons in general.

Can't National Assessment exercises be used elsewhere for purposes of testing?

Yes they can, since all released exercises are public property and in form are indistinguishable from test items. To convert from assessment to testing, one need only administer all exercises to given individuals, then sum up the total score of each individual and compare it with the total scores of others in the group, in familiar achievement-test fashion. Or one may compare the average total standing of one

Facts about National Assessment

group with that of another group, for example, the average scores made by the students in each building in a local school system. The important question here is not *can* the National Assessment items be used to test individual achievement, but *should* they be—would it be valid or invalid, wise or unwise, to utilize NAEP exercises locally for achievement and accountability testing. This question is discussed more fully later in this booklet.

Do NAEP results falling below a certain percentage indicate failures of learning or teaching?

Not at all. This too is an important point. In developing exercises, NAEP sought to ensure that no individual items would yield either all correct or all incorrect responses. The advance field testing and the mix of easy and difficult items were undertaken so that educators examining the percentage results could gain a sense of the range of knowledge of differing levels of difficulty that different-aged persons possess. Naturally one may interpret the NAEP percentage results as one wishes. But the intention and design of the assessments were such, however, that no lower-limit expectations were set. A 20 percent correctness level on one item, for example, counts as neutrally as an 80 percent correctness level on another. Therefore, as teachers accustomed to classroom testing, we must take care, in studying National Assessment results, to set aside our usual assumption that results below 60 or 70 percent are indicators of failure and cause for alarm.

How do the various subgroups identified by NAEP compare on the three English assessments?

National Assessment publishes numerous reports in all subject areas comparing each subgroup with the national percentage on an exercise-by-exercise basis. Looked at in the most generalized manner possible, average correctness levels across exercises in the several English assessments confirm what for many readers will be stereo-typical expectations.

1. Region (national quadrants). The Southeast region falls roughly 4 percent (i.e., percentage points, here and hereafter) below the national level, the Northeast about 2 percent above it, while the Central and West do not differ from the national figure.
2. Sex. Females tend to score 2 percent above the national level, males 2 percent below it.
3. Color (nonblack and black). Nonblacks do not differ from the national figure, whereas blacks tend to score about 15 percent below that level.
4. Parents' highest educational level (four categories). Young people

whose parents received no high school education fall 10 percent below the national level. Those whose parents had some high school fall 5 percent below, and those whose parents are high school graduates do not differ from the national figure. Those whose parents attended school beyond high school average 5 percent above the national level.

5. Size and type of community (seven categories). Young people from extreme inner city schools average 10 percent lower than the national level, and those from extreme rural schools 4 percent lower. Those from schools in the suburban fringe score about 2 percent higher than the national figure, and those from extremely affluent suburbs (professional and managerial parents) score 6 percent higher. Students from schools in small cities, medium-sized cities, and the rest of big cities do not differ from the national level.

What has been the response to the English assessments?

Several statements apply here. Most professional articles have been directed at the writing assessment, the majority being critical of its design features. The attempts of popular education writers to sensationalize National Assessment findings have thus far proved short-lived. A number of statewide assessments have been conducted wherein state totals are compared with the NAEP national figures. Local school districts increasingly are following suit, often to settle issues of educational funding. NAEP itself, in response to professional criticism, either has redesigned or is redesigning both objectives and exercises for its second-cycle assessments in the three English areas. Generally speaking, a healthy dialogue on testing and assessment has ensued within the profession.

How may further information about National Assessment be obtained?

National Assessment has issued a great many official reports on the three assessments summarized in this booklet, some of which are mentioned herein as being especially useful to teachers and researchers in the English language arts. NAEP also maintains a bibliography listing various articles, reviews, and booklets written about any of the ten assessments, and itself publishes a bimonthly *NAEP Newsletter*, which highlights the progress and results of ongoing assessments and provides information about the utilization of National Assessment exercises at the state and local levels throughout the nation. A catalog listing National Assessment reports and other materials in print, plus a no-cost subscription to the newsletter as well as answers to requests for additional information about Assessment programs and services, may be obtained by writing:

National Assessment of Educational Progress
700 Lincoln Tower
1860 Lincoln Street
Denver, Colorado 80203.

Specific reports issued by National Assessment are available and should be ordered from:

Superintendent of Documents
U.S. Government Printing Office
Washington, D.C. 20402.

Chapter Three

The Writing Assessment

Despite the rise of visual studies and broadsides announcing the post-literate society, writing, the second R, continues to be viewed by teachers and nonteachers alike as one of the most important subjects taught in school. Paradoxically, however, there is widescale disagreement on its curricular definition. What do we teach when we teach written composition? How do we measure the outcomes of our teaching? What is writing as a school subject, and what are its objectives and content?

Typically, in the day-to-day world of actual teaching, we avoid confronting these questions head-on, allowing our classroom practice to speak for itself and answer by implication. Some of us even suppose that in the end, once the public pronouncements have been uttered and the classroom doors closed, everyone else believes and teaches the same way we do. But the truth is that everyone does *not* think the same way about the teaching of composition. One of the contributions of the first National Assessment of writing, apparent in the responses of the profession to its objectives and exercises, has been to underscore this fact and bring it to the fore, thus forcing us to examine our unstated assumptions about the teaching of writing.

The Writing Objectives

Objectives for the first writing assessment were developed by the Educational Testing Service (ETS) under contract to National Assessment. ETS staff members first proposed five possible categories for assessment—general, personal, social, scholastic, and vocational writing. A seven-member panel of educators then reduced these to four actual objectives, which were subsequently reviewed and approved by eleven lay panels in various parts of the country. Following are the objectives in final form:

1. write to communicate adequately in a social situation (letters, directions, formal notes, addressing envelopes, invitations);
2. write to communicate adequately in a business or vocational

situation (information and application forms, mail order letters, business invitations, formal letters);
3. write to communicate adequately in a scholastic situation (notes and announcements; narrative, descriptive, and expository essays);
4. appreciate the value of writing (recognize the value of writing; write as a normal course of behavior; receive satisfaction from writing).

Despite the diversity of input into the development process, it is clear that the objectives measuring proficiency (the first three) pertain exclusively to utilitarian writing. In terms of familiar although inexact dichotomies, this means that the Assessment viewed school writing as expository rather than creative, communicative rather than expressive, extensive rather than reflexive. British educators might describe the same thing as writing that is transactional and casts the writer in the role of participant in the world's affairs, rather than imaginative writing casting one in the role of spectator or recreative onlooker. However we label these opposing kinds of writing, the important thing to bear in mind from the outset is that while the first writing assessment included one important kind of writing, it excluded another kind considered at least equally important by a great many teachers. Fortunately this exclusion has been compensated for by the objectives and exercises used in the second-round assessment.

The Writing Exercises

Once the writing objectives were decided, ETS personnel under NAEP supervision formulated a body of exercises measuring the extent to which each objective had been attained by students at the several age levels. Three kinds of exercises were used:

1. acceptable/unacceptable exercises: short writing tasks scored "acceptable" or "unacceptable" according to whether or not the writer included certain required items of information; used with objectives one and two;
2. yes/no exercises: questions of beliefs or facts responded to by a "yes" or "no"; used with objective four;
3. essay exercises: topics requiring fully developed compositions, each rated by two trained readers on a scale of 0 (blank page) to 8 (best) on the basis of overall quality; used with objective three.

Altogether there were ten acceptable/unacceptable exercises used at one or more of the three age levels, sometimes with differing content (but the same basic writing task) deemed most suitable to a given age. There were nineteen yes/no questions asked, though not at all age levels. The nine year olds and thirteen year olds wrote three

16   The Writing Assessment

essay exercises each, and the seventeen year olds two. All exercises were administered by means of written directions accompanied by the playing of a tape-recorded reading of their text. This arrangement prevented the intrusion of reading problems into the writing assessment and provided respondents with written directions for reference while writing.

Acceptable/Unacceptable Exercises

The ten acceptable/unacceptable exercises presented writers with an imaginary background situation, then directed them to write a short passage pertaining to that situation. Following are two examples of the full exercise exactly as given to respondents:

Letter of Invitation (Age 13; number 3 in Table 1)

About three months ago, Leo Logan moved from the city to the country. His father bought a farm, and now Leo's address is Rebel Road, Rural Delivery No. 1, Harris, Nebraska 69000.

Leo likes the country, but he misses his old friend Ozzie Drake. Leo's mother says, "Why don't you write to Ozzie and invite him to visit us for a week this summer?"

Write Leo's letter of invitation to Ozzie.

[Approximately 1–1½ pages of lined space were provided for the response.]

Recording a Telephone Message (Age 13; number 4 in Table 1)

You are going to hear a telephone conversation between two boys, Al and Ben. During the conversation, you will discover that Ben is going to have to write a note to his mother. Listen carefully to find out the things that Ben will have to say in his note. [Children then listened to the conversation reproduced below. It was *not* printed in the children's booklet.]

Al: Hey, Ben, this is Al. I called you to remind you you're supposed to come down to my house for supper tonight before the game.

Ben: Oh yeah, I remember. Your mother and father are going to pick me up on the way back from the barber shop. What time do you think you'll get here?

Al: Oh, around 5 o'clock.

Ben: O.K. I'd better leave a note for my mother. She won't be home until 5:30 and maybe she's forgotten that I won't be eating at home.

Al: You'd better remind her of the ball game, too. She's supposed to pick us up afterwards, isn't she?

Ben: That's right. Your father is taking us to the game but my mother is bringing us home. Thanks for reminding me. I'll write the note right away.

The Writing Assessment

You will now have another chance to hear the conversation between Al and Ben. Listen to it carefully again and then, when the boys have finished talking, write the note that you think Ben should leave for his mother.

[Approximately ½ page of lined space was provided for the response.]

Table 1 indicates in abbreviated fashion the content of all ten acceptable/unacceptable exercises rank-ordered by average correctness level from least difficult to most difficult. To be scored acceptable, each response had to meet all the conditions mentioned under "requirements" in the description of the exercise. As is apparent from the foregoing samples, however, respondents were not specifically informed of these requirements, since part of what the exercises measured was, for example, the knowledge of what a letter of invitation or a recorded phone message should contain.

The other exercises reported in Table 1 were also presented in elaborated forms similar to the samples above. The mail-order exercise (item 7) depicted an advertisement for aquarium sea horses, while the envelope-addressing and information-blank tasks (items 5 and 8) gave respondents outline drawings of an envelope and an information blank to be written on. (Note: In Table 1 and all following tables, a horizontal line in place of a numerical percentage means that the particular exercise was not administered to the age in question.)

Two problems with the acceptable/unacceptable exercises immediately come to attention. One is that the tasks required of the respondents were more in the nature of information processing than they were compositional. Verbally given content was, in effect, merely re-expressed rather than directly composed out of the writer's own thought and intentions. A second aspect is that, in processing the given information, respondents had to do so from the point of view and role assigned in the exercise. In almost every case, these were other than their own, much as if they were acting as a scribe for someone else, or role-playing on paper.

The net effect was that these short writing exercises were almost certainly more difficult for students at all ages than essentially the same rhetorical tasks would be if they were to arise naturally and realistically in the students' own lives. If nine year olds know, for example, that their class is holding a pet show in the gymnasium at 4:00 next Wednesday, surely more than one in five can express this fact in a written sentence or two—all that was required in item 10.

Similarly, it seems reasonable to believe that more than half of the seventeen year olds can describe accidents that have really happened to them (item 6), or can compose a single mail-order statement (item 7) directing a company to send them a certain product,

Table 1
Ten Writing Tasks Scored Acceptable/Unacceptable

Abbreviated Description of the Task	Percentage of Respondents Scored Acceptable at Each Age Level		
	Age 9	Age 13	Age 17
1. Thank-you letter: requirements: letter form addressed to grandmother, readable, express appreciation	88	—	—
2. Describe a process or procedure: requirements: free choice of a familiar process, list all steps with full or partial specificity	—	—	75
3. Letter of invitation: requirements, age 9: letter form, express invitation, state day, time, and place of school play	35	91	—
requirements, age 13: letter form, addressed to friend Ozzie, include invitation for a visit			
4. Record a telephone message: requirements, age 9: state message pertaining to a meeting of two people, plus place, time and day	31	67	79
requirements, age 13 and 17: include three items of information pertaining to dinner, transportation arrangements, outing			
5. Address an envelope: requirements, age 9 and 13: include and properly place name, street address, city and state, of both sender and person sent to	28	78	—
6. Describe an auto accident diagrammed in an accident-report form: requirements: state name of street, direction, traffic-light status for each car, plus facts of collision while each was turning	—	—	53

7. Mail-order letter: requirements: state that sea horses are the product wanted, plus sender's full address	—	46	55
8. Fill in a personal information blank: requirements, age 9: full but fictitious name as provided, plus full address, zip, full birth date, today's date requirements, ages 13 and 17: as in age 9, plus sex, height, weight, hair color, eye color	16	26	61
9. Business letter of invitation: requirements: invite mayor to speak at school, name the school, suggest topic, discuss the choice of dates	—	27	—
10. Announcement of school event: requirements: state that there is to be a pet show, give place, time and date	21	—	—

giving their name and address. In the business letter of invitation (item 9), the thirteen year olds had only to write "I would like to invite you to speak about your job to my class at Saluki Junior High, whenever you can come." Assuming a composition task of this sort in real life, it is difficult to believe that only one eighth grader out of four could carry it out successfully; two or even three seems more likely, though not everyone will agree with this supposition.

In short, one plausible interpretation of the acceptable/unacceptable exercises is that, in addition to writing, they also required of students the cognitive operations necessary to process the information given and maintain the role and point of view assigned. This extra activity made the exercises more difficult than real composition would have been, presumably for all age levels. It was hardest for the nine year olds, as seen in the uniformly low correctness totals for this age, perhaps because most of these children are still prisoners of egocentrism in the psychological sense and lack the ability to stand apart from and effectively monitor their ongoing language productions. Thus one might very well conclude that the obtained correctness levels in Table 1 are in fact considerably lower than the actual percentage of students who in real life could perform the rhetorical tasks simulated in the exercises.

Yes/No Exercises

Table 2 sets forth the percentage of "yes" responses to a number of questions pertaining to self-sponsored out-of-school writing. These questions were designed to measure the fourth writing objective, "appreciate the value of writing."

Table 2
Percentage of "Yes" Responses to Questions about Writing

Question Asked	Age 9	Age 13	Age 17
Are there jobs requiring much writing?	—	89	—
Have you ever sent writing in for publication?	—	17	—
During the past year have you:			
left someone a written message?	—	61	86
written a letter ordering a product by mail?	—	—	54
Other than in school have you ever written:			
a song lyric?	—	50	50
a story?	23	58	54
a poem?	18	47	64
a joke?	41	—	—
Other than in school have you ever written:			
a play?	—	26	18
a report?	17	—	—
a newspaper story?	—	11	17
a magazine article?	—	10	11
If on a trip last year, did you write:			
a thank-you to someone visited?	30	36	—
a letter about the trip?	25	39	—
notes on the places seen?	27	32	—
a post card?	23	42	—
a letter while on the trip?	25	39	—
a report about the trip?	20	27	—
a trip diary?	7	10	—

As with any baseline data reported in isolation, we have no standards of comparison in terms of which to interpret the figures above, only subjective judgment. We might wish that the assessors had asked all questions at all ages, since this would have given fuller indication of cross-sectional trends across the three age levels. It is clear, however, and a matter worthy of concern, that although both of the four-year periods see significant additional numbers of young people writing poetry on their own, almost no additional students undertake for the first time the writing of songs, stories, plays, or articles between their thirteenth and seventeenth years. Perhaps high-schoolers simply grow more set in their ways, successfully resisting the motivational blandishments of their instructors. Or perhaps our motivational techniques need improving.

On the other hand, it ought to be a source of positive comfort and encouragement to English teachers to note that poetry leads all other kinds of self-sponsored writing among high school seniors and that fully half of all thirteens and seventeens claim to have written both stories and poems on their own outside of school. Many teachers would have estimated far lower percentages. Certainly these facts impressed the professionals who helped revise the writing objectives for the second-round assessment, since the latter makes ample provision for imaginative expressive writing (see Chapter Six of this booklet).

Still others, however, will interpret the percentages in Table 2 as severely inflated, arguing with some plausibility that most young students cannot remember very reliably what they have written over a one-year period, or whether they did it on their own or as a school assignment. And for many people, young or old, it is always easier and more pleasant to answer "yes" rather than "no" to questions of this sort. In the end, of course, readers are free to attach whatever interpretations they believe appropriate to the data in Table 2.

Essay Exercises

Seven essay topics were developed for use at the three age levels. The topic assignments are shown below exactly as they were given to respondents:

Essay Topics for Age 9

Going to School
Think about what happens when you go to school. Write a little story that tells what you do from the time you leave where you live until you get to school. Be sure to include everything that you think is important.

Forest Fire
Here is a picture of something sad that is going on in the forest. Look at the picture for a while. Do you see the forest fire? Write a story about what is happening in the picture. This is an important story because you want people to know about this sad event. [The picture depicts a forest fire with animals swimming across a river rapids to obtain safety.]

Astronaut
Here is a picture of an astronaut on the moon. Look at the picture for a while and think about what is happening. Now, pretend

that YOU were the astronaut, and write a story about your walk on the moon.

Essay Topics for Age 13

Pen-pal Letter
Write a friendly letter to a "pen pal" in another country, telling him (or her) about your preparations for some holiday. Your letter should be as "newsy" as possible because your friend probably does not know how you do things where you live.

Historical Event
If you could make an event in American history happen again so that you could play a part in it, which one would you choose? Write a composition in which you describe the event and explain why you chose that particular event and what part you would like to play in it.

Famous Person
Most of us look up to some famous person as a representative of the things we believe in or as the kind of person we would like to be. This person may come from any part of our society. For instance, we might admire Winston Churchill or Martin Luther King, Walter Schirra or Mickey Mantle, Florence Nightingale or Barbra Streisand. No matter where this person comes from or what kind of work he or she does, however, we can recognize such traits of greatness as determination, physical courage, the ability to inspire others, and faithfulness to some worthy cause. Think about a famous person whom you admire. Select a particularly admirable characteristic or quality of that person—such as Mickey Mantle's courage in the face of crippling physical handicaps or Florence Nightingale's determination to fight against strong governmental pressure. Write an essay of about 200-250 words describing this characteristic or quality. Be sure to provide an illustration of it from the person's life. Try to show that the person is great at least partly because of this characteristic or quality.

Essay Topics for Age 17

Tomato Lady
Here is a picture of a woman with some tomatoes. Look at the picture for a while and decide what is going on. When you have decided, write a story that tells what is happening in the picture and what is likely to happen next.

Famous Person
[Topic identical to that used at age 13.]

Holistic Scoring of Essay Responses

Each essay was rated for overall quality by two trained readers using a 0 (blank page) through 8 (highest quality) scale, with their two ratings summed to yield a 0 through 16 scoring range. This method of rating overall quality is ordinarily termed "holistic," a name derived from its emphasis on a reader's impression of the whole piece of writing rather than independent aspects of the whole, such as style, content, mechanics, and so on.

Holistic scoring techniques have been extensively researched over the past twenty years, particularly by personnel of ETS in connection with essay exercises used in various College Board examinations. It is known, for example, that inter-rater reliability correlations (measures of the extent to which raters agree with one another on the rating assigned to a given essay) reach as high as .70 to .80 and above if raters are given special training sessions prior to their work.

Equally high correlations are found between initial ratings and delayed reratings of a given essay by the same reader (after special training), thus verifying intra-rater consistency. Put more simply, we know that trained readers are consistent in their own overall-quality ratings and agree with the ratings of other readers about two thirds of the time. This is a far higher percentage than we initially thought, on the basis of earlier studies of judgments of writing ability, could ever be attained.

Two key requirements of holistic scoring should be remembered if one is to fully understand the process. First, raters must judge individual essays relative only to the other essays in the group being rated rather than to outside norms. Raters must use all rating categories certain minimum percentages of the time, on the proven assumption that the general quality of any large collection of essays will distribute itself normally, that is, in familiar bell-shaped fashion. Second, a rater is never permitted to base a rating entirely on any one aspect of the essay being read, no matter how outstandingly good or bad it may seem, but must always attend equally to all aspects—usually identified as content, organization, style, expression, and mechanics. This means, for example, that an otherwise mediocre essay may not be assigned the highest rating because the writer happened to succeed in deftly maintaining a humorous style. Nor may an essay reasonably well written in all other regards be given the lowest rating just because the writer apparently lacks control over mechanical matters. Such is the logic of holistic scoring. Teachers may wish to reflect on the differences and similarities between this method of evaluating writing and procedures ordinarily used in the classroom.

Results of the Essay Exercises

Once the holistic scoring was completed, the assessors rank-ordered the essays sorted by topic and age and assigned the designations "high quality" to those at or above the 85th percentile of the overall-quality score distribution, "middle quality" to those clustered around the 50th percentile, and "low quality" to those below the 15th percentile. Although it is unclear what criteria of typicality they used, the assessors identified the following essays as "typical" of the three quality levels at each age:

Age 9, Forest Fire Essay

High quality:
There was a fire in the woods one day. It was burning the trees down and burning the grass. It was a real big fire. There was a river near by but there wasn't any body to put it out. There were rocks in the water. There were dear swimming across the river to get away from the fire. There was a raccoon on a rock try to get across. The fire was getting biger and biger. The water was runing down a small hill. (85 words)

Middle quality:
Once upon a time there was a big forest there was 400 acres of trees and thonands of animals. but one day the forest caught a fire tree's was burning down and falling there was 2,000 firemen fight the fire, blazes was going 300 feet high in the air in two weeks the hold forest burned down a killed 500 hundred animals and 100 men and burned down 8,000 trees, and that was the end of the great forest fire (80 words)

Low quality:
Some one have been caralss a drop a mach. a starch a forest fire. And one in the picture it show two deep. Gone is to the watch and corn to. and I see a deep a watch fall. and I see rock. And I see the tree our fire. And a tree. And I see a the two a fathr and mother. The Eand (63 words)

Age 13, Famous Person Essay

High quality:
   I admire Pres. John F. Kennedy for his courage and dermination, especially in the face of an emergency. This is important for a man in the position of President. He must be couragous and stand up for his convictions, as well as the convictions of the people.
   If he were to panic in the face of stress and political pressure, or make a wrong decision, the whole country could be in trouble.
   Courage is an admirable trait, but you don't have to fight lions to have courage. Courage is standing up for what you think is right, no matter what other people think or do. This is an important quality for a man in president Kennedys' position.
   I think one of the things that best illustrate courage in President Kennedys life was the Cuban missile crissis. By standing up for our country President Kennedy proved he had courage. He didn't panic, when the Communists sent missiles to Cuba. He remained cool and told them to get their missiles out of Cuba. The Russians

said they would if Kennedy got the missile sites out of Turkey. Kennedy said no, get your missiles out of Cuba.

Kennedy showed strong determination in handling this crissis. He could easily have started a war by doing the wrong thing, and by standing up for his beliefs, he prevented what could have been a Russian stronghold. He said things the way he wanted them, and he wasn't Wishy-Washy. This kind of courage is a trait everyone should have. (253 words)

Middle quality:
I like Deacon Jones as a football player. He plays for my favorite team the Rams. He plays Defensive End. He is I think 250 pounds 6'-7". I like football very much and just like the way he plays. He always makes a quarterback worry. He aways makes key tackles. In one game I saw him in, he caused three fumbles. He is a great atheletic. He is a ten year pro. I don't know how many allstar games he has played in, but I know he has played in they. Here in Southfeild, Mich they had a radio program on and they had football questions on they asked who was the best team in the N.F.L. they said the Rams, they asked who was the best Defensive End in the N.F.L. they said Deacon Jones. Deacon Jones is my best football player and I guest thats all I have to write about him although he might not be that famous he's my favorite. Defensive men might not get known that good but he dose. (174 words)

Low quality:
Martin Luther King Jr.

He was a famous man who did not believe in violence just peace and brotherhood. he was a democratic person and a minister. he help serve his country. he was a negro person who had a lovely family and when he died or rather before he did. he stated I've reached the mountain top He also made a longer speech But i can't really say it all and his friend Jesse Jackson was also like him too and also another great man. Reverend Avernathy these were three great non-violence people. (91 words)

Age 17, Famous Person Essay

High quality:
Sammy Davis Jr.

I admire Sammy Davis Jr. because his qualities are numerous both in courage and acting.

His courage comes in when he was on the road with his father and his uncle. That's the part of him I admire the most. Without any definite job or any stationary place to sleep. He and his gaudian had plenty of determination and willpower. Sammy knew that one day he would finally reach a place among his fellowman not as a black servant but as an equal brother to all of mankind. This goal he has already achieved. He has come, all the way, through dismal days, foodless days and shelterless nights. He knows what is to suffer. He knows what it is to be hungry. But the fruits of labor can be so wonderful. Now he is a loved man among men.

Sammy Davis Jr. has the ability to sing, dance, act and make friends. Sammy has dazzled every audience he has ever performed for with his God-given talent. With all of these qualities, how can anyone do anything but admire a man like that. (183 words)

Middle quality:
Ben Franklin is an admirable character. Inventor, statesman, scrntist and ambassador were what he is renown for.

Although he never became president, he had more than his share of influencing America. His scientific achievements and inventions alone would make his famous for all time.

His political achievements also immortalized his. He also aided America by rescueing foreign relations in France.

His character impressed many great men of Franklin's time. Presidents, statesmen and other prominant people asked his advice and seeked his counsel.

He lived in an important time in history for America. He played a good part in the Declaration of Independence.

His discovery of electricity was phenomenal in the scientific world. Other small contributations like the wastebasket, eyeglasses, pot stove.

His persistence in life and his organized way of doing things enabled him (along with his genius) to do so much for America.

We all have something to learn from him. (152 words)

Low quality:
I think that Present Kenndy was a famous person before he was shot he was going to try and stop the war in Vietnam because of all the people killed and the boy that were dying so young. He wasn't like the other men that ran for presendet against him they all say that they were going and ty to stop the war there but I lot of them just do that so people think that he is the man for our county, But in my eyes there nothof but a fony. But I think Prisent Kenndy wasnt he tried and I think sooner or later he would of stop the was there. An another thing he tried to stop the Negros from stop soitey ad get along with the red white people ad a Nego should be able to walk in a restrant ad get served. (148 words)

Obviously, many more sample compositions than these are required to represent the flavor and range of the style, content, and rhetorical approaches found in the 2000 essays actually written on each topic. In view of this, the assessors compiled a collection of over 3000 essays from all age groups and printed their texts exactly as written under the title *Writing Report 10: Selected Essays and Letters.* Persons who examine Report 10 almost without exception comment on the extreme variability of its contents and cite the need to read a great many compositions on any given topic in order to gain an adequate sense of the writing that topic produced.

The Uses of Holistic Scoring

Returning to the question of holistic scoring of the essay items, one notes that a number of English teachers who have criticized the writing assessment in professional journals have hit hard at the idea of merely ranking essays by overall quality, arguing that it tells us nothing whatever about pieces of writing other than the fact that some are generally adjudged superior to others. The point seems well taken, at least on its face. Inasmuch as blank-page responses received 0 ratings, there remained a 2 to 16 scoring range for each essay actually written. So the net effect of the scoring process was simply to sort all essays on a given topic into fifteen categories of overall quality, from poorest to best.

Remember too that the score assigned to a given essay is meaningful *only* in relation to the other essays comprising the group in which it was rated, and not in relation to external standards. To illustrate the extent of the intragroup relativity involved in holistic scoring, let us suppose that 125 essays out of a group of 2000 rated holistically have received the top-quality rating of 16. If these 125 essays are then considered as a separate group complete unto itself and are rerated by the same readers under the same procedures, they will receive new ratings ranging in a near-normal distribution from 2 through 16, with no more than five or six receiving the top-quality rating that all had formerly been assigned.

In light of these facts, two questions arise. Why did NAEP use holistic scoring at all? And why did it not, either additionally or instead, use a procedure that would have yielded independent substantive descriptions of the various ways certain writers have written? The answer to the second question is that the ETS personnel simply didn't know how to characterize free writing except to rank order it by quality level, since rank-ordering and not substantive description is the main business of ETS and the College Board. Fortunately, more precisely worded topics and alternative scoring procedures have recently been developed by writing teachers acting as consultants to National Assessment. These are being utilized in the second-round writing assessment and are discussed later in this chapter.

In answer to the first question, however, holistic scoring is by no means as indefensible as some have claimed. Everything depends on the purpose and method of its use. NAEP chose to employ the procedure in preparation for the comparisons it expects to make between the quality of first-round assessment essays and that of writing produced in subsequent rounds by equivalent samples of young people. The process works as follows. After assigning essays to quality rankings, the assessors compile a full-range sample from the assessment in question, which is then pooled with a similar sample from another assessment. The pooled essays are treated as a single set to be rerated as a whole, with the initial ratings and identifications of assessment time concealed. This means that the essays written in one assessment compete for the higher ratings on the 2-to-16 scoring scale against essays from the other assessment. If the papers from one time are significantly better than those from another time, they receive a significantly greater proportion of the high ratings. In other words, the procedure enables the assessors to answer in a perfectly valid manner the question their mission requires them to ask: Has the writing produced at one point in time grown poorer or better than the writing produced at some earlier time?

The 13–17 Overall-Quality Comparison

At the end of the first writing assessment, of course, no other essay scores existed, so cross-time comparisons of the sort just described could not be made. But because the thirteen year olds and the seventeen year olds both wrote the "Famous Person" essay, a direct comparison of overall quality between the two age groups was possible. Full-range samples of papers from each age group were pooled and rerated with the age designations and initial ratings concealed. In other words, the raters knew only that they had a single fresh group of essays to rate holistically. They did not know that the group consisted of essays written by different aged students, or that the essays from the two age levels were thus competing for the higher ratings. The results of this comparison are surprising, and rather unpleasantly so.

On the average, as one would expect, the essays of the seventeen year olds received the higher ratings. The trouble lay at the ends of the distributions in the two age groups. Results showed that 5 percent of the thirteens wrote essays judged to be as good as or better than those of the top 15 percent of the seventeens. In other words, for every three of the best writers at age seventeen there is one at thirteen who writes just as well. At the lower end of the distribution, 84 percent of the thirteens wrote essays as good as those of the top 86 percent of the seventeens. This means roughly that for each of the poorest writers in the lowest fifth of the age-thirteen group, there is one seventeen year old in the lowest fifth of his or her age group who writes just as poorly. Remember, in the present instance this does *not* mean that the bad writing in each age group is bad relative only to its own group. Rather it means that the bad writing of the seventeens is *absolutely* as bad as that of the thirteens, since papers from the two ages now comprise a single rating group. And the two are, quite literally, indistinguishable.

Consider how a longitudinal interpretation of these facts (i.e., an interpretation based on the assumption that the essays were written by the same group of students over the four-year interval between ages 13 and 17) raises doubts about the efficacy of composition instruction in the high school years. One out of three of the best writers (top 15 percent) in their senior year, though still one of the best, has made no progress or advancement in absolute terms since entering grade nine. At the opposite extreme the situation is worse, since the poorest writers (bottom 15 percent) have made no improvement whatever in four years. They are still poorest in their group, and in absolute terms have made no advancement.

One can see the headlines now: "High School English Not Reaching One-Third of Gifted Students," or "Poorest Writers Learn Nothing in Four Years of English." Facetious as they may sound on first reading, these statements contain more than a little truth and should not lightly be dismissed. To be sure, the conclusions are based on a single composition written for National Assessment. But unless one believes that unknown factors produce dramatic variations in the levels of writing ability attained by different generations of seventeen year olds, it is difficult to refute the longitudinal interpretation just given, especially when one remembers the representative sampling procedures used by NAEP. Thus we are left with the disturbing evidence that at least some of the best high school students are understimulated by the writing curriculum, and that there is wholesale stagnation throughout the high school years among the least able writers.

The Study of Writing Mechanics

Not wishing to ignore matters of detail, the assessors further characterized one set of essays from each age level in terms of what we ordinarily call "mechanics." Results of the study were published separately as *Writing Report 8: Writing Mechanics*. Data for this report was gathered from the "Forest Fire" essay written by the nine year olds and the "Famous Person" essay written by the thirteens and seventeens. Instead of analyzing all essays, NAEP assembled samples of high quality, middle quality, and low quality writing at each age level. These were defined as papers close to the 85th, 50th, and 15th percentiles respectively. Because of their shorter length, more essays from age nine were required to equalize the word-size of the samples:

Approximate Number of Essays in Each Sample:	Age 9	Age 13	Age 17
High Quality:	525	225	175
Middle Quality:	725	250	325
Low Quality:	350	150	150
Total:	1600	625	650

Three kinds of procedures were employed in characterizing the mechanics of these essays:

1. computer counts of 24 quantifiable features of texts, such as average word and sentence lengths, numbers of each kind of punctuation mark, misspellings of certain words the computer had been programmed to look for, and so on;
2. generalized prose characterizations of specific mechanical strengths and weaknesses of writing typical of the three quality levels at each age, prepared by panels of recognized experts;
3. error counts of each of eight familiar types of errors, performed by teams of experienced English teachers. Two teachers working independently counted a given error type in each paper, and their totals were averaged.

Readers wishing to examine the computer-count data and the prose characterizations, both of which are quite voluminous, will need to consult the full *Writing Mechanics* report.

This report begins, incidentally, with three fairly brief paragraphs (found on pages 1 and 2) summarizing the findings of the mechanics study, particularly the prose characterizations. These paragraphs state among other things that nine year olds "have limited competence in sentence construction and restricted vocabularies," that the lowest quality essays of the thirteens indicate "that the writers had no knowledge or understanding of the conventions of written language," and similarly, that the poorest writing of the seventeens was produced "by teenagers who have no real grasp of the conventions of written language."

As many readers will recognize, it is exactly these statements and a number of others from the opening paragraphs in the *Writing Mechanics* report that continue to be quoted whenever a popular education writer decides to stir up concern about the supposed low level of writing ability among schoolchildren. For example, writing in the April 1974 *Reader's Digest*, Vance Packard stated the following in reference to the findings of NAEP's writing assessment:

> Its first national sampling of nearly 100,000 Americans was an eye opener. By age 13 only the best of the students could cope with the basic conventions of writing. (This was after eight years of schooling!) By age 17 about half the students could put together simple sentences and express simple ideas in general, imprecise language; but three quarters of them misspelled at least one word, and more than half made errors in choice of words.

Insofar as it should be obvious to intelligent persons that elementary and junior high school students naturally have a great deal still to learn about writing the language, it is fair to conclude that these introductory statements from the *Writing Mechanics* report have

The Writing Assessment

hindered far more than they have helped ongoing attempts to place the results of the writing assessment in proper perspective.

Table 3 reports the number of errors identified per hundred words of writing in eight error categories. Rather surprisingly, one notes that familiar orthographic errors such as capitalization faults or sentence fragments do *not* decrease from presumably high levels among nine year olds to markedly lower levels among seventeen year olds. Except for spelling, where a 50 percent reduction occurs over each four-year period, the number of errors of a given type is more or less constant across the three ages.

Table 3
Number of Mechanics Errors per 100 Words of Writing

Age	Quality	Spelling	Punctuation	Capitalization	Fragments
9	high:	4.6	1.9	0.9	0.6
	middle:	6.5	2.2	1.1	0.6
	low:	12.2	2.5	1.7	0.6
	average:	8	2	1	1
13	high:	2.3	2.2	0.8	0.6
	middle:	3.5	2.9	1.1	0.6
	low:	5.8	3.5	1.7	0.8
	average:	4	3	1	1
17	high:	1.2	2.1	0.6	0.5
	middle:	1.9	2.5	0.7	0.6
	low:	3.6	3.1	1.0	0.8
	average:	2	3	1	1

Age	Quality	Run-ons	Awkward Construction	Agreement	Incorrect Word Choice
9	high:	1.0	1.1	1.3	2.3
	middle:	1.2	1.2	1.4	2.8
	low:	1.6	2.6	1.7	3.6
	average:	1	2	1	3
13	high:	0.6	1.1	0.9	1.5
	middle:	1.2	1.5	1.3	1.8
	low:	1.7	2.5	2.4	3.1
	average:	1	2	2	2
17	high:	0.6	0.9	0.9	0.9
	middle:	0.6	1.3	1.2	1.4
	low:	1.6	1.8	2.5	2.9
	average:	1	1	2	2

"Average" indicates the number of each error-type for the given age, averaged across the three quality levels and rounded to the nearest whole number.

How is one to interpret the information in Table 3? Conventionally, teachers assume that errors occur at a high rate among the youngest writers, then steadily taper off to near zero incidence during high school. Thus it is claimed that much drill and practice on error correcting ought to be required of younger writers to reduce the high initial incidence of error as soon as possible. Except for spelling, however, National Assessment results indicate that this high initial error rate is in fact nonexistent. Thus, although some editing and directed proofreading is essential at all ages, there seems little reason to continue to give students in grades five through seven the especially large doses of error-correcting practice they typically receive.

Mechanics in Perspective

One might well ask, as high school teachers often do anyway, whether the foregoing results indicate that it is possible to eliminate the incidence of virtually all mechanical error by grade nine. The answer is no. The level error rate from ages thirteen to seventeen is certain to continue no matter how much or what kind of practice students receive before age thirteen. This is because the characteristics of their written language are changing during this interval, so that the nature of the errors committed also changes. We know that their writing grows more syntactically complex, and errors of punctuation and awkward construction are bound to occur in sentences the high school student was incapable of writing when younger and only now is learning to handle.

For example, since noun phrases used as subject grow more elaborated and are more often paralleled, the occasions for agreement errors and faulty parallelism naturally increase. Older students are choosing words from ever-expanding vocabularies and in the process quite naturally choose wrongly in the case of newly and still only partially-learned words. Furthermore, many of the so-called run-ons and fragments may result from purposeful stylistic decisions, as they do in mature professional writing. And so on. Even though the errors of the older students are categorically similar to those of younger ones, their nature differs in the ways just mentioned. Although we obviously ought to be concerned about the apparent lack of growth among the poorest writers as indicated by the overall-quality evidence in the 13-17 comparison, the error data just discussed may be interpreted in general as a sign of healthy ongoing learning.

Altogether, the National Assessment findings on writing mechanics, although based on only a fraction of the writing collected, suggest three conclusions. First, they put to rest the belief that fourth graders are up to their ears in error compared with older students and thus need a diet of drill drill drill during the intermediate grades, to the exclusion of other kinds of activities that might expand their language and thought.

Second, the NAEP findings also remind us that error cannot be eradicated before the high school years because older students will be experimenting with kinds and forms of language they could not have attempted at all when younger. Naturally they will make errors in the process, errors which could not have been prevented by advance drill. High school teachers should rejoice at the growth of writing ability these more sophisticated errors bespeak, gladly teach about them, and resist all temptations to accuse middle school and junior high teachers of not doing their jobs.

Third and finally, we must keep the issue of writing mechanics in perspective, remembering that mechanical error counts are relatively specific; the categories can be defined, the data easily obtained. It is equally easy in the classroom to find such errors. Control of mechanical conventions is of course desirable, but it represents a minor part of writing. Sometimes the ease of getting the information leads people to overstate its value. We cannot say whether the number of errors reported in Table 3 should be viewed with alarm, for that depends upon more than mere counts of error. We have no information as to how many of the errors may have inhibited understanding, and how many might have been eliminated in a writing situation which encouraged later proofreading and revisions. Everything considered, the writing assessment produced insufficient evidence to justify our diverting additional instructional time from more fundamental problems of thought and expression to mechanical matters.

Assessing Writing and Teaching Writing

Overall, the writing assessment yielded four kinds of information—one, a survey of attitudes and experiences; two, mechanical error counts; three, some data about skill in processing conventional information and role-playing while writing; and four, a body of prose essays ranked according to quality. The survey may stand as a model for classroom use, as long as we bear in mind the admonitions that one must always deal with the students who are at hand and that the value placed on writing by members of each particular class must always be assessed anew. The data on errors and information processing has already been discussed. The main point to remember is how small a part of writing these things really are. The results of the essay exercises, however, invite interpretations directly applicable to the writing classroom.

Here it is important to bear in mind a point that is often missed entirely. It is simply this, that problems arising in the assessment of *is this said with any degree of reservation?*

34 The Writing Assessment

writing are very often equally present in the teaching of it, since in their forms the two activities, teaching and assessing, are in large measure identical. In teaching writing one sets a topic, then comments on the results by describing the writer's successes and failures at every level, ranging from overall quality to the narrowest mechanical matters. In assessing writing, as we have just seen, one does exactly the same thing. Only the purposes differ—that of teaching is tutelary, whereas that of assessment is the measurement of attainments. In short, we teach writing largely by assessing it, and the lessons we can learn from problems encountered in assessment used in measuring are applicable also to assessment used in teaching.

One problem with the NAEP essay exercises, which is also a problem in classroom teaching, is that the assessors seem to have underestimated the arduousness of writing as an activity and consequently overestimated the level of investment that unrewarded and unmotivated students would bring to the task. After all, the students were asked to write by examiners whom they did not know. They were told that their teachers would not see their writing, that it would not influence their marks or academic futures, and presumably that they would receive no feedback at all on their efforts.

Clearly this arrangement was meant to allay the students' fears, but its effect must have been to demotivate them to some degree, though how much is anyone's guess. We all know that it is difficult enough to devote a half hour's worth of interest and sustained effort to writing externally imposed topics carrying the promise of teacher approbation and academic marks. But to do so as a flat favor to a stranger would seem to require more generosity and dutiful compliance than many young people can summon up. Readers are strongly urged, if at all possible, to examine Report 10 and to decide for themselves the motivational level of the writing it contains.

In any event, one can never overstress the importance of motivation in the teaching or assessing of writing. Answering multiple choice questions without reward in a mathematics assessment or a science lesson may be one thing. Giving of the self what one must give to produce an effective prose discourse, especially if it is required solely for purposes of measurement and evaluation, is quite another. Yet how often do we as classroom teachers merely "give out" composition assignments to students, with no more thought to their motivational levels than that they *will* write simply because they *have* to?

Formulating Composition Topics

Another problem common to both teaching and assessment pertains to the structure and wording of topics. Taken together, those used in the writing assessment give eloquent testimonial to the difficulty of formulating such topics in clear rhetorical terms that specify

*the hazards of "topic setting"
(Unet ETS!)*

purpose, mode of discourse, voice, and audience in such way that the compositions of different writers may be compared with one another and judged accordingly. The terms just mentioned may strike some readers as technical and removed from classroom realities. But consider the assessment results. It happens that each of the age-nine topics, all of which ask for "stories," were construed quite variously by the writers. On the "Going to School" topic, for example, some writers developed fantasy occurrences while others stuck to the mundane facts of daily life. Some wrote about a real happening they had once seen, such as a traffic accident; others gave maplike directions for getting from home to school; still others merely described scenes along the way. The words "sad" and "important" in the "Forest Fire" essay led some writers to downplay what was happening in an attempt to express and describe their feelings. Others tried to explain why forest fires constitute important events, and a few ventured into the Smokey Bear idiom and wrote essays on fire prevention.

The thirteen year olds in the "Pen-pal Letter" divided in their sense of audience towards the pen pal, as between those who fancied that they shared mutual background experiences, and those who did not. Some concentrated on the holiday while others interpreted "newsy" to mean write a diarylike letter. The "Historical Event" topic tended to be treated as three essay questions to be answered in series—What was the event? Why did you choose it? What part would you like to have played in it? The "Famous Person" topic, unlike the others, was so overstructured that words and entire clauses from the topic itself kept showing up in the students' essays. The "Tomato Lady" narrative was interpreted equally diversely. Some writers fantasized freely while others looked for clues in the picture and produced detective-style ratiocinative essays. Some interpreted the scene dramatically while others merely enumerated the objects depicted. Of those who projected into the future, some related a single culminating event while others set forth a plotted sequence of events. A few invented a life condition for the woman in an attempt to explain *why* she was doing whatever they thought she was doing in the picture.

Taken in the aggregate, the writing produced on each of the NAEP essay topics was diffuse and unfocused as to discourse structure and devoid of a single sense of audience and unified voice and tone. In an instructional situation, of course, one can deal with each paper individually in terms of the interpretation its writer placed upon the topic as given, no matter how vague its formulation. More often than not, however, we as teachers have one or another reading of the topic in mind, fail to recognize its ambiguities, and tend unconsciously to penalize students who happen to take it differently.

This is bad enough in the teaching of writing; but when measurement is the purpose, whether in the classroom or in National Assessment, one finds that there are no common features of the writing on which to judge and compare, other than overall quality at one extreme and mechanics at the other. Imprecisely formulated topics prevented National Assessment from measuring students' ability to handle specific rhetorical tasks defined in terms of mode, purpose, voice, and audience. The same thing often happens in classroom measurement of writing, one suspects, and it is precisely here that composition teachers can learn valuable lessons from the weaknesses of the first writing assessment.

Granted, many important features of writing other than mechanics are reflected in overall-quality judgments of a rhetorically diverse body of writing: varied sentence structure, vocabulary, fluency and aptness of word choice, consistency of tone and style, clarity of organization, and unified and logical idea content, to name the most obvious. These things can be judged in a set of compositions regardless of whether they result from one precisely focused topic, one imprecise topic construed diversely, or multiple topics. What cannot be judged except in the case of the focused topic, however, is the writer's ability to handle a defined rhetorical task stipulated (once again) in terms of mode and purpose of discourse, sense of audience, and speaking voice. Furthermore, even "unity" and "organization" change meaning when used with different forms of discourse.

When topics are carefully formulated, two things become possible. One, scoring rubrics can be developed such that a group of essays can be evaluated in light of the primary rhetorical trait contained in the topic. These scoring rubrics can guide the individual classroom teacher as well as the national rater. Second, NAEP would thereby acquire a body of rhetorically homogeneous writing from different age levels that could be examined by researchers in light of any number of basic but pressing questions pertaining to children's development of abstraction levels, organizational skills, rhetorical distancing, "de-centering" in the Piagetian sense, and a host of other compositional abilities as well.

In light of the foregoing, it is encouraging to note that the still unreleased second-round writing assessment, in addition to including expressive writing and decreasing the percentage of acceptable/ unacceptable exercises, also employed topics formulated with primary-trait scoring in mind and provided for the development of the scoring rubrics themselves. The second-cycle results are scheduled for release in 1976, although there is some uncertainty about the availability of funds to carry out the primary-trait scoring. Nonetheless it is important to remember that second-round topics *were* formulated with the attainment of rhetorical specificity and homogeneity in mind, even if scoring and research on the results must be delayed.

Summary

First of all, teachers everywhere should applaud the fact that NAEP elected, even in its first-round writing assessment, not to employ the multiple-choice questioning format so widely used in commercial tests of writing ability. Equally enlightened was the recognition that the information it gathered is baseline data. No prior norms or absolute standards were invoked, nor should they be, except subjectively, by persons interpreting the assessment findings.

We ought to be especially heartened too by the fact that NAEP stopped short of scoring entire essays on an acceptable/unacceptable basis in order to report the percentages of each. Given the imprecise wording of the essay topics and the rhetorical diversity of the writing they elicited, such a scoring procedure would have been ridiculous. Primary-trait scoring in the future will in fact permit acceptable/unacceptable scoring, though with much greater sophistication. We will need to be very careful not to use it simplistically.

Finally the general question must be asked. What does the writing assessment show about the composition ability of students? The answer has several parts. There is reason to believe that the seemingly low percentages on the acceptable/unacceptable exercises (addressing envelopes, writing orders, filling in information forms, etc.) are seriously deflated, owing to the pretend role-playing required by the exercise topics. Holistic scoring of essays plays an important role in establishing comparisons between groups or across time, but provides no substantive description of the writing so scored.

The level of skill in mechanics gives no cause for alarm, and the summary statements in the *Writing Mechanics* report are better off forgotten. The overall-quality comparison of thirteen year olds' writing with that of seventeen year olds, though limited to a single essay, cannot be ignored. Clearly we need to invent new methods of teaching writing to the poorer writers during their high school years. Assuming that one accepts a longitudinal interpretation placed upon one-time data, the results indicate the failure of current practices in this area.

Last, the NAEP reports tell us little else about the nature of the essays collected, beyond whatever experiential sense of their content we may gain from *Report 10*. We have, of course, grown increasingly aware of the need to further refine our instruments of measurement— in this case, by defining a taxonomy of rhetorical tasks in light of which individual essay topics and accompanying primary-trait scoring rubrics can be precisely formulated.

Yet the implications for teaching are clear. There is no need, based on assessment findings, for a headlong rush to incorporate into our courses lessons on filling in forms and taking telephone messages. At least not until we establish that young people cannot do these things for real.

Further, we need to recognize that mechanical error will occur in the writing of students of all ages as a sign of learning in progress. We should be impressed by the fact that as many as half of our students by their high school years have engaged in self-sponsored out-of-school writing, and should encourage them in whatever ways we can.

Perhaps most importantly, we should recognize that "writing ability" spans a wide range of rhetorical occasions, and we should attempt to formulate topics with enough precision to enable student writers to experience as many of these as possible. Doing so would also permit us as teachers, for tutelary purposes, to assess writing in ways that would lead to the development of heightened proficiency by each student.

In other words, from the failure of National Assessment to provide precisely formulated topics, we recognize how important it is not to make a similar mistake in our own efforts. To the ancient maxim of composition teaching, that any writing is preferable to none at all, we can now add the corollary truth, that a variety of certain definable kinds is preferable to just any.

Chapter Four

The Reading Assessment

Nearly everyone considers reading the single most valuable academic skill that schooling imparts to young people. Nothing is surer to alarm parents, for example, or more genuinely terrify teachers and administrators than the prospect of a decline in children's reading scores. Reading has received more monies from federal programs of compensatory education than all other subjects combined. "Right to Read" is more than merely a slogan or the name of a government project. It is, like the right to a livelihood and a guaranteed income, a right that Americans in the latter third of the twentieth century have come to regard as universal and inalienable. Thus it is not surprising that National Assessment considers reading its highest priority subject and intends to assess it most often and most extensively.

One result of the in-school emphasis on reading is that teachers are quite familiar with tests of reading achievement. Most of us have seen these tests and received printouts of our students' scores. Many of us have administered reading tests and participated in the process of selecting them for schoolwide use. We know about the skills and subskills these tests measure, about their diagnostic use, and about the grade-level scores they report.

But the reading assessment is not an achievement test. It does not compute summed scores of any kind (raw, standardized, percentile, stanine, or grade level) for individual students, or for groups of students comprising educational units at any level. Nor is it a diagnostic measure. Because there are no independent norms or scores of prior assessments with which to compare them, the national correctness percentages for the nearly 200 reading exercises must be viewed as baseline data only. They stand in isolation, devoid of any context except their own, considered in the aggregate.

Clearly, then, we must prepare to examine the NAEP reading exercises and their results from a wholly unaccustomed perspective. We need not become preoccupied by our usual question about how well students are reading. In fact, we are not permitted to address the question at all with regard to the NAEP data, except in the realm of subjectivity, where one person's opinion is more or less as valid as another's. Thus we may enjoy, for once, the liberating luxury of bypassing the "how well" question and of thinking instead about what happens and why in the act of reading and the taking of reading tests. How are test questions answered? What language has to be read? How difficult is it? What makes it difficult? What do tests really tell us? Hopefully, from a consideration of these questions, we may deepen our understanding about the things that are important in the teaching of reading.

The Reading Objectives

The first five objectives of the reading assessment, developed in accordance with National Assessment procedures by panels of teachers and lay persons, were as follows:

1. Comprehend what is read:
   a. read individual words,
   b. read phrases, clauses and sentences.
   c. read paragraphs, passages, and longer works.
2. Analyze what is read:
   a. be able to trace sequences,
   b. perceive the structure and organization of the work,
   c. see the techniques by which the author has created his effects.
3. Use what is read:
   a. remember significant parts of what is read,
   b. follow written directions,
   c. obtain information efficiently.
4. Reason logically from what is read:
   a. draw appropriate inferences from the material that is read and "read between the lines" where necessary,
   b. arrive at a general principle after examining a series of details,
   c. reason from a general principle to specific instances.
5. Make judgments concerning what is read:
   a. relate what is read to things other than the specific material being read,
   b. find and use appropriate criteria in making judgments about what is read,
   c. make judgments about a work on the basis of what is found in the work itself.

Strictly speaking, only the first objective pertains to reading per se, since the thought processes mentioned in the others are used in listening to language equally as much as in reading it. Nonetheless, they are thought processes we expect our students to develop in school, usually as a result of reading instruction. And all five objectives typically occur in reading programs and tests of reading achievement. A sixth objective, "have attitudes about and an interest in reading," was not assessed, although questions about students' reading habits and preferences were asked as part of the literature assessment (see Chapter Five).

No sooner had NAEP finished developing exercises for the first-round assessment, based on the foregoing set of objectives, than it began to convene groups of consultant reading specialists to revise these objectives for the second-round assessment. Readers are invited to contrast the first-round objectives with the newer ones, which appear in Chapter Six of this booklet. The differences are quite noteworthy.

The Reading Themes

Following the completion of the reading assessment, in preparing to write their official reports of findings, NAEP staff members decided that an alternative structure would be more meaningful than the original list of objectives as categories for reporting the assessment exercises. Thus they developed a framework of "themes," worded as follows:

1. understanding words and word relationships (literal comprehension of isolated words, phrases, and sentences);
2. graphic materials (comprehension of the linguistic components of drawings, signs, labels, charts, maps, graphs, and forms);
3. written directions (comprehension of directions, plus ability to carry them out operationally);
4. reference materials (comprehension and knowledge of indices, dictionaries, alphabetizing, and TV listing formats);
5. gleaning significant facts from passages (comprehension, and to a limited extent, recall, of literal content in the context of a larger reading passage);
6. main ideas and organization (ability to abstract upwards from the sentence-by-sentence content of a passage and recognize main ideas and organizational features);
7. drawing inferences (ability to reach a conclusion not explicitly stated in the passage, in most instances relying only on information given but in a few cases on knowledge unrelated to the passage);
8. critical reading (ability to recognize author's purpose, and to understand figurative language and literary devices).

The official NAEP documents, plus reviews of the reading assessment that have appeared in professional journals and elsewhere, tend to discuss the reading results in terms of these themes rather than the actual objectives. The summary of results presented in this booklet does so as well. Notice that themes two through four (graphic materials, written directions, and reference materials) refer to types of reading matter, whereas the remaining ones constitute a hierarchy of cognitive skills, each of which more or less depends for its pursuit upon mastery of those preceding it.

The Reading Exercises

Of the total of all exercises administered in the reading assessment, just under 200 have been released, that is, made available for public inspection. (The unreleased exercises are being re-administered in the second-round assessment.) Some of the released exercises pertain to isolated phrases and sentences of text, while others ask about the content of approximately fifty short passages of prose and poetry.

Most of the questions were in multiple-choice form, though a handful called for responses such as drawing lines or diagrams, or writing answers in longhand. All but a few allowed the respondent to look back into the given reading passage to search for the correct answer. Additionally, two reading passages were given respondents at each age level from which reading rates were computed, and five recall questions were asked on each to obtain a measure of factual comprehension related to rate.

Answering Multiple-Choice Exercises

As teachers we are thoroughly familiar with the format of multiple-choice questions in reading tests. These questions are usually based upon a given reading passage and consist of the question "stem," as it is called, followed by the correct answer inserted somewhere within a list of three or four incorrect answers, called "distractors." Persons answering multiple-choice questions assumedly read the given passage plus the question stem and then figure out which is the correct answer from among the distractors. But how does this "figuring out" process work?

Let us consider the following multiple-choice item, shown here exactly as it appeared in the reading assessment:

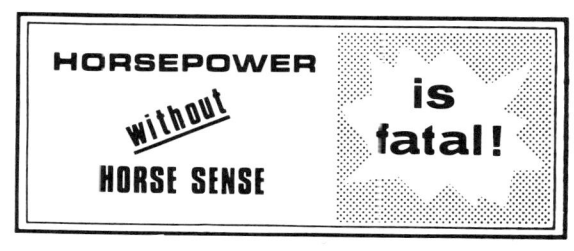

> **HORSEPOWER** without **HORSE SENSE** is fatal!

Where would you probably see this sign?
On a gymnasium floor
At a racetrack for horses

The Reading Assessment   43

> On a highway
> In a grocery store
> I don't know

In this case, the reading passage consists of a single sentence shown as it might appear on a signboard. Assume that the respondent reads the passage (i.e., recognizes its words and comprehends their grammatical relations within a sentence) as well as the question stem and the possible answers. What then takes place is an unconscious mental process in which the passage, the question stem, and the correct answer are combined by means of grammatical transformations into the equivalent of a single sentence, as follows: You would probably see the sign "horsepower without horse sense is fatal" on a highway. The reader then mentally assesses the content of this single sentence as to its truth value—is it true or not true? To know the meanings of its words (of which, presumably, "horse sense" would be most difficult for students) and to comprehend its grammatical structure is, quite obviously, to confirm its truth. In other words, in assessing the sentence as true, the reader verifies that the phrase "on a highway" is the correct answer to the question and that the distractors are merely irrelevant.

As a second illustration of this process, consider the following item. In this case as in most of the NAEP exercises, only certain parts of the reading passage need to be included in the mentally constructed sentence:

> Sleeky and his mate found their way to Miller's pond one fall day. It was a cold day and very, very clear. The sun shone on the bright fall leaves. It made the water look silver. Both otters were swimming down the stream that ran into Miller's pond. . . .
>
> How many otters were there?
>
> Two
> Three
> Four
> Five
> Six
> I don't know

Here the reader returns to the passage and notes the phrases "Sleeky and his mate" and "both otters." These are then combined with the question stem and, if they are literally comprehended, with the correct answer "two." Thus the full sentence cognitively processed and assessed for truth value in the correct answering of the question is: "Sleeky and his mate" and "both otters" mean there were two otters.

Readers obviously use a variety of search strategies and shortcuts to locate in a given reading passage the material necessary to complete the constructed sentence and confirm the correct answer. And reading through the passage word-for-word is only one of these strategies, a fact well known to teachers who have closely observed students taking multiple-choice tests, or asked them how they go about answering the questions.

Remember too that the process used in the answering of multiple-choice questions is, like most thought processes, inaccessible to conscious introspection. A linguist might explain the matter as follows:

> The transformational constructing and truth testing of sentences is a mentalistic activity hypothesized to explain the language-based cognitive operations persons clearly perform, not only in answering multiple-choice reading questions but in a large share of verbal thinking in general. Although illustrations of the process are typically given in worded surface structures, its technical description must be formulated in terms of unvocalizable deep structures only abstractly related to the surface manifestations of language.

To pursue the matter further, however, would be to dive deeper into the murky seas of psycholinguistics than our intellectual breathing apparatus could tolerate.

Presentation of the Results

To prepare the results of the reading assessment for presentation within manageable limits, the author of this booklet began with the exercise questions as administered by the NAEP examiners, then transformationally combined the appropriate parts of each into a single sentence of varying content and complexity. This was the sentence the reader had to construct in mind and assess for truth value in order to answer the question correctly.

These sentences, capsulizing and displaying the assessment content, are of three kinds—18 imperative sentences requiring literal comprehension only, 104 declarative sentences requiring literal comprehension only, and 59 declarative sentences requiring literal comprehension plus an inference of some sort going beyond its literal content.

Admittedly this is an unorthodox approach to reporting the nature of test exercises. The author developed it for use in this booklet in hopes that it would give reading teachers new insights into the unconscious thought processes used in answering objective test items, whether multiple-choice format or any other. Notice that the approach focuses attention on the item of language (the sentence) we *know* the reader had to construct mentally and then comprehend, as distinct from the remainder of the reading passage and the distractors, which the reader *may or may not* have read and comprehended, either fully or partially.

Some persons will of course want to see the exercises as given. These are presented in National Assessment's *Report 02-R-20, Released Exercises*. Those who wish to examine the reading passages from which the constructed sentences were extracted will find many of these passages included in Appendix A of the present booklet.

In looking over the tabled information presented on the next several pages, readers should try to keep the following points in mind:

1. Each sentence presented in the tables represents a single assessment exercise.
2. A horizontal line in place of a numerical percentage means that the exercise was not administered at that age level.
3. The theme to which each exercise was assigned is named in parentheses beneath the reported sentence, sometimes together with other descriptive information.
4. Parenthetically quoted titles name the reading passage on which the exercise was based and indicate that the text of the passage is included in Appendix A.

Literal-Comprehension Sentences

The sentences requiring literal comprehension are shown in Tables 4 through 7, rank-ordered from highest to lowest percentages of correct responses. There are obviously a great many sentences to consider, and readers will wish to peruse them selectively and at leisure, thinking about possible sources of difficulty as reflected in the correctness percentages given for each age level.

The sentences listed first were obviously the easiest to read. For the most part, these easy exercises contained no reading passage, and consisted only of a question stem, a set of five possible answers, including the phrase "I don't know." The interpretive commentary following each table was prepared by the author of this booklet and is not taken from official NAEP reports. Readers are invited to agree or disagree with this commentary and to make additional interpretations of their own.

Except for the bug spray, poison ivy, and recipe sentences, all of the imperative items required the respondent to perform the operation named in the sentence. Only the five-step drawing sequence proved difficult. Some of the thirteen year olds apparently could not read "horizontal," and mistakes early in the sequence made other errors inevitable later on. Low totals on the final item, for example, may have resulted from inability to read "vertical" or "triangle," or from the fact that the respondent simply didn't have a triangle to work with in step five, owing to earlier mistakes.

Clearly the vocabulary in the poison ivy sentence was difficult for nine year olds, some of whom probably stopped reading at "dermatitis." The low totals for the recipe item are puzzling. The passage

Table 4
Literal Comprehension Sentences, Imperative Mode

Item of Language Read and Comprehended	Percentage of Respondents Scoring Correct Answers at Each Age Level		
	Age 9	Age 13	Age 17
Write the number 3 in the large circle. (written directions)	—	98	—
Write the number 5 in the large square. (written directions)	—	97	—
Write the number 7 in the large triangle. (written directions)	—	97	—
Write the number 4 in the small circle. (written directions)	—	97	—
Write the word "cat" on this line. (written directions)	93	98	—
Write the number 2 in the small square. (written directions)	—	96	—
Hold can approximately 10 inches from surface. (written directions; can of bug spray)	—	92	—
Connect the dots to make a solid line. (written directions)	84	95	—
Fill in the oval below the figure that can be made with just three lines that cross each other. (graphic materials; array of geometrical figures)	89	—	—
Connect the dots to make a solid line. (written directions)	82	93	—
Draw a line connecting 2 and 7. (written directions)	80	95	—
To avoid ivy dermatitis once a person is exposed to poison ivy, wash all exposed areas within about five minutes of exposure. (significant facts; passage describing treatment of poison ivy)	41	77	85

After softening the yeast in the water, combine the next four ingredients — milk, sugar, salt and shortening. (written directions; recipe format — ingredients list followed by directions) — 22 38

Note: The following five items were given sequentially as a single exercise in the written directions theme:

1. Draw a horizontal line near the bottom of the page. — 86 93

2. Draw two circles approximately one inch in size above the line which just touch each other and the line. — 67 84

3. Draw another circle of the same size above the first two which just touches both. — 75 88

4. Now connect the centers of the three circles with straight lines. — 50 72

5. Draw a vertical line from the top of the triangle in the picture to the line you drew first. — 44 68

consisted of a recipe for English muffins presented in recipe format, wherein yeast and water were the first two ingredients vertically listed, followed by milk, sugar, salt, shortening, and flour. The question stem and the recipe directions were worded as shown in Table 4, and all the respondent had to do was look back into the ingredients list, note the four ingredients listed after yeast and water, and find these in the multiple-choice listing. Yet four out of five thirteens seemed unable to do this, as did two out of three seventeens. At least they didn't do it. Perhaps they couldn't, perhaps they simply wouldn't. One wonders.

Table 5 indicates that over half (53 of 104) of the declarative literal-comprehension items were processed at or above an 80 percent correctness level, averaged across ages. Except for the items about the film guarantee, which were read only by the seventeen year olds, the sentences tended to be short, simply worded, and concrete. Crucial vocabulary items presumably were words such as "pedestrians," "cafeteria," "principal," "ferocious," "bicyclists," "detective," and so forth, most of which were recognized and comprehended even by the nine year olds. Four out of five young children were able to abstract the main idea of a 36-word passage about Colorado mountains and the 73-word passage "Sports Cars." Most students were

Table 5
Declarative Literal-Comprehension Sentences Lowest Difficulty
(80 to 98 percent average correctness level)

Item of Language Read and Comprehended	Percentage of Respondents Scoring Correct Answers at Each Age Level		
	Age 9	Age 13	Age 17
You would find information about *earthworms* on pages 195-196. (reference materials; reading an index)	—	—	98
The sign "pedestrians only" shows where walking is permitted. (graphic materials)	—	—	98
The name of the bear pictured in the advertisement is Smokey (significant facts; name written on Smokey Bear's hat)	—	95	98
A boy might look for the sign "bus stop" if he needed to take a bus home. (graphic materials)	97	—	—
"Classroom" is a compound word made by joining two words together. (written directions)	93	98	—
You would find science news on page 51. (reference materials; reading a table of contents)	—	95	96
A "cafeteria" is a place where you might go for lunch. (words and word relationships)	95	—	—
The person in charge of a school is a "principal." (words and word relationships)	95	—	—
"Has the answer already been given?" asks a question. (words and word relationships)	—	92	96
"A sign is hanging on the door" best tells what the drawing shows. (graphic materials)	89	98	—
If you have *never* visited the moon, fill in the oval here. (word and word relationships)	92	94	—

The Reading Assessment 49

Hope is the town closest to Centerville. (graphic materials; reading a roadmap)	85	96	99
It should come as no surprise to learn that 9 out of 10 Americans are in debt. (significant facts; factual information in larger passage)	—	90	94
"Mystery" best describes the kind of television show this one is. (reference materials; reading a TV guide)	—	—	92
This is a game for the whole family, adults as well as children. (written directions)	—	91	93
The writer tells you how sports cars differ from passenger cars. (main ideas; "Sports Cars")	84	—	99
You can drive all the way from Northtown to Falls City on Highway 71. (graphic materials; reading a roadmap)	82	95	98
The sign "pedestrians use crosswalk" tells you what to do if you are walking. (graphic materials)	87	97	—
The drawing shows that the fish looks as if he is going to eat the worm. (graphic materials)	88	96	—
"Maybe it was because of the three old women" means there were three women in the room when James awoke. (significant facts)	—	88	93
"Sleeky and his mate" and "both otters" mean there were two otters. (significant facts)	—	91	—
"Inside this cage is an extremely ferocious animal" tells you that there is a dangerous animal inside the cage. (words and word relationships)	85	96	—
"The dog on the leash has spots on it" best tells what the drawing shows. (graphic materials)	85	95	—
The first dealer is chosen by each player drawing a card from the deck and the player with the highest card becoming dealer. (written directions)	—	88	92

continued

Since color dyes may change in time, this film will not be replaced for, or otherwise warranted against, any change of color. (significant facts)	—	—	90
The advertisement tells you to be sure to drown all campfires. (significant facts)	—	86	92
The boy wanted a new ball. (words and word relationships)	88	—	—
The student did best in foreign language. (graphic materials; reading a report card)	—	80	94
These grades cover the first reporting period. (graphic materials)	—	82	92
"3:00 p.m." means this program is presented in the afternoon. (reference materials; reading a TV guide)	—	—	86
By car Northern is not closer to Rice Lake than to Hope. (graphic materials: reading a roadmap)	79	85	95
It started to rain and the fog grew thick, so the weather was wet. (significant facts)	86	—	—
The maximum amount for which this policy covers medical payments is $1000. (graphic materials)	—	84	88
This film will be replaced with an equivalent amount of unexposed Filmo film if found defective in manufacture, labeling, or packaging, or if damaged or lost by us or any subsidiary company even though by negligence or other fault. (significant facts)	—	—	85
Maybe it was because he had been thinking about how to run away from school when he went to bed the night before. (significant facts)	—	81	89
The sign "bicyclists use street" shows where you should ride your bicycle. (graphic materials)	69	89	96

The Reading Assessment

"Master detective (Bob Johnston)" means Bob Johnston plays the master detective in the movie. (reference materials; reading a TV guide)	—	—	85
Any number of people may play the game. (written directions)	—	77	93
It was a cold November Monday means the story takes place in the month of November. (significant facts; recall of information)	—	85	84
What happened *first* in the story is that the wind pushed the boat farther and farther out to sea. (main ideas; factual content of longer passage)	83	—	—
The person who said "I like stories about spies" likes spy stories. (critical reading)	75	90	—
2 Super Mutt—cartoons are shown at 2:00 p.m. (reference materials; reading a TV guide)	73	84	92
How heavily, is borne out by government statistics which show that income has increased 50 percent—while debts have increased 110 percent. (significant facts)	—	76	89
This person gives three reasons for wanting a dog instead of a cat for a pet. (main ideas; organization of longer passage)	83	—	—
When a player has used up all his cards, he drops out of the game. (written directions)	—	82	84
Centerville is not farther west than Hope. (graphic materials; reading a roadmap)	72	84	95
It was a cold November Monday in Brooklyn means the story takes place in the city of Brooklyn. (significant facts; recall of information)	—	82	81

continued

If you like books which are *not* about people, you would read *All about Elephants*. (reference materials)	73	88	—
Frangibles communicated by thought waves. (significant facts; "Frangibles")	—	—	81
Bubble gum that never loses its sugary flavor would stay sweet for a long time. (graphic materials; reading a bubble gum wrapper)	65	95	—
Each player draws a card from the deck and the player with the highest card becomes the first dealer. (written directions)	—	76	93
"I *certainly* won't miss that movie" means I'm going to that movie. (words and word relationships)	—	76	83
This passage is *mainly* about the mountains in Colorado. (main ideas)	80	—	—

familiar with the conventions of roadmap printing. The TV guide percentages are lower than might be expected, apparently more because of the special typographic format than the language *per se*. It appears generally true that the items of language in Table 5 were not particularly difficult for children of any age and thus reveal little about the limits of their language-processing abilities.

Keep in mind that the sentences presented here contain the actual questions asked in the reading assessment. They appear as statements only because they have been transformationally combined with information constituting the correct answer to each. Every sentence is formed in such a way that if the readers doing the assessment exercise could read and fully comprehend its content, they could automatically (that is, without further thought) give a correct response to the question as asked. Assumedly, then, the primary cause of incorrect answers was not that the respondents were led astray by the multiple-choice distractors, but rather that they were unable to read and/or comprehend and/or mentally construct the full sentence, whereupon their choices among the distractors became essentially random.

Table 6 contains several items that a majority of nine year olds cannot process. They were unable to abstract upwards to a statement of main idea about the "Farmer Brown" passage. The sentences about

Table 6
Declarative Literal-Comprehension Sentences, Middle Difficulty
(60 to 89 percent average correctness level)

Item of Language Read and Comprehended	Percentage of Respondents Scoring Correct Answers at Each Age Level		
	Age 9	Age 13	Age 17
The thing that Silky the Spider hated most was rain. (significant facts)	79	—	—
A hindfoot caught/In the button box/ Buttons/Scattered in all directions. (significant facts; lines of verse)	77	81	—
The phrase "quick clamps" is a good one to describe the eyes of this creature because it suggests the eyes' rapid shuttering movement. (critical reading; "Turtle Poem")	—	—	77
The prince and the princess getting married is like Mary and the young man getting married. (main ideas; comparison of concluding events of two stories)	66	88	—
"Chatter" means talk to one another. (words and word relationships)	—	76	—
The heat wave resulting from the explosion of a one-megaton nuclear weapon can cause moderately severe burns of exposed skin as far as 12 miles from the point of detonation. (significant facts)	—	72	78
In the telephone book you would find Mr. Jones between Johnson and Judson. (reference materials)	63	86	—
Her tours of the United States, Europe, and Asia meant that the extent of Miss Keller's lecture tours was only on three continents. (significant facts; "Helen Keller")	—	72	78

continued

The poet asks for the following three things in this order: a ship, sailing weather, companionship. (main ideas)	—	—	75
This story is *mainly* about a stormy day at sea. (main idea; "A Stormy Day")	75	—	—
65% crude protein is more protein than 20% crude protein. (graphic materials; dog food label)	67	81	—
To tell your class about windmills, the best book to use would be an encyclopedia. (reference materials)	57	90	—
If there is a tie for high card, the trick remains in the center and the winner of the next round wins these cards also. (written directions)	—	62	86
After graduation, Helen began to study the problems of the blind. (significant facts; "Helen Keller")	55	83	82
"Wind whistled woefully" tells how something sounds. (critical reading)	73	—	—
Fever, chills, headache, and sore throat tell how you look and feel when you get scarlet fever. (significant facts)	45	82	91
Of all the things to eat in the world, Silky the spider liked bean soup the best. (significant facts)	72	—	—
It was a cold November Monday means the story takes place on a Monday. (significant facts)	—	70	73
English muffins are baked on top of range on medium-hot greased griddle. (written directions)	—	66	75
Highway 20 does not run on the south side of Rice River (graphic materials; reading a roadmap)	52	71	86

The Reading Assessment

The pair of words "whistled-wailed" best suggests the sound of wind blowing. (critical reading)	70	—	—
Paragraphs II and III in the passage are written from a personal point of view. (critical reading; "Skiing")	—	55	78
This student is improving in his work in science. (graphic materials; reading a coded report card)	—	53	80
The reason a sports car can turn a corner more easily than a passenger car is that it is built smaller and lower. (significant facts; "Sports Cars")	42	69	89
Calamine lotion can be used to sooth the discomfort of itching, burning skin. (significant facts)	33	79	85
What Amos did *first* in the story was take his lunch to the park. (main ideas)	65	—	—
To begin the game, the player to the left of the dealer plays first by placing the top card from his stack face up in the center of the table. (written directions)	—	60	68
The main idea of the passage is that all living things are affected by living things. (main ideas; "Farmer Brown")	27	75	91
Most fatal accidents occurred between 2 a.m. and 3 a.m. (graphic materials; reading a graph)	—	54	74
Children's Variety Repeat means the program is being run a second time. (reference materials; reading a TV guide)	37	68	84
The program on Channel 6 at 3:00 p.m. is an hour (60 minutes) of popular music. (reference materials; reading a TV guide)	59	61	69
A surface burst causes much more immediate danger from radioactive fallout than an air burst. (significant facts)	—	55	68

calamine lotion and scarlet fever were not processed by half of the youngest children, either because the word meanings were unknown or the spellings were unrecognizable or both. Over half of the nine year olds could not interpret "for these reasons" as relating back to the preceding sentence in the "Sports Car" passage. That the TV-guide sentences were difficult for these children seems strange; presumably the difficulty lay in the special printing format used in TV guides and reproduced in the test item. The roadmap sentence was negative in truth-value and contained two location names. Doubtless it posed problems not of literal comprehension but rather, for nine year olds, of operationally identifying the places named on the map given. The "Helen Keller" sentence occurs about three-fourths of the way through this fairly difficult 171-word passage and perhaps was not reached by many nine-year-old readers. Or the word "graduation" may have been the stumbling block for others, just as the word "encyclopedia" clearly was in its sentence.

For thirteen year olds, the line graph showing auto fatalities was a challenging exercise whose difficulty (unlike that of most of the other graphic materials) was *essentially* graphic rather than linguistic. The report card item assumed knowledge that "LIFE SCI" meant "science" and required the student to read a numeral in the "Citizenship Comments" column, then look up the statement associated with that numeral in a list headed "Citizenship Comments Code." The fact that the item in question pertained to academic standing, not citizenship, may have confused some students needlessly. The point-of-view problem in the "Skiing" passage probably indicates that thirteen year olds are ready for but also in need of overt instruction in this concept.

It is easy to imagine why the "if . . . then" sentence describing rules of a card game and containing the word "trick" was difficult for thirteen year olds. It is less easy to understand why the short and simple sentence telling who plays first in the card game was slightly more difficult, just as it seems strange that only 60 percent of the thirteen year olds could process the phrase "an hour of popular music" in a TV guide as being the equivalent of "60 minutes." The three-paragraph passage describing air, surface, and subsurface nuclear explosions was complex and difficult, and the statement about the surface burst had to be compiled from sentences remote from one another in the passage. Understandably, it was correctly processed by only half the thirteen year olds and was the most difficult item in Table 6 for the seventeen year olds. The last TV-guide sentence, quite surprisingly, was almost as difficult for the seventeens as for the younger ages.

The sentences in Table 7 were of greatest difficulty. Note that the independent clauses (T-units) in the four tables become considerably longer as one moves from the less difficult to the more difficult sen-

Table 7
Declarative Literal-Comprehension Sentences, Highest Difficulty
(Below 60 percent average correctness level)

Item of Language Read and Comprehended	Percentage of Respondents Scoring Correct Answers at Each Age Level		
	Age 9	Age 13	Age 17
The winner is determined in that the point of the game is for a single player to collect all of the cards. (written directions)	—	45	72
The best way to find out if there is something about Eskimos in a book is to look in the index. (reference materials)	48	68	—
According to the paragraph, the origins of the word "beat" are obscure. (significant facts; "Beat Generation")	—	51	64
Admiral Drake sent a penguin in answer to Mr. Popper's letter. (significant facts)	57	—	—
It takes about 30 minutes to bake English muffins on top of the range. (written directions)	36	66	65
Wet packs of boric acid are helpful in case of severely poisoned eyelids and swollen eyes. (significant facts)	21	65	76
You would most likely find this paragraph in a collection of essays. (reference materials: "Beat Generation")	—	39	67
Immediately after the passage discusses the use of penicillin to treat scarlet fever, it tells that the disease may be accompanied by infections of the ear and throat, inflammation of the kidneys, pneumonia, and inflammation of the heart. (main ideas)	—	43	63
One method the poet uses to attract the reader's interest is an unusual point of view. (critical reading; "Turtle Poem")	—	46	53

continued

"The moon slipped in and out from behind the clouds like a blinking flashlight" means that the author compares the moon to a flashlight. (critical reading)	33	65	—
The title which tells the *most* about this story is "Easter Eggs in the Past." (main ideas; "Easter Eggs")	26	54	64
The passage also points out the importance of the fact that any change in the environment is likely to cause other changes. (significant facts; "Farmer Brown")	25	69	—
You would look under the heading "cinema" to locate the reviews of a current movie. (reference materials)	—	26	62
"Thy sweet love remembered" saves this man from wishing to be different than he is. (drawing inferences; Shakespearean sonnet)	—	30	52
You would probably see the sign "Horsepower without Horse Sense Is Fatal" on a highway. (critical reading)	23	45	76
The author presents the story of Helen Keller in chronological order. (main ideas; "Helen Keller")	6	24	58
The *main* point of this paragraph is the definition of the word "beat." (main ideas; "Beat Generation")	—	29	27
"Budgetism" could *best* be defined as having oneself precommitted to regular, unvarying monthly payments on all the major items. (words and word relationships; "Suburbanites")	—	18	25
The maximum amount this policy would pay in case you injured another person is $25,000—bodily injury liability, $25 thousand each person. (graphic materials)	—	8	19

tences. For imperative sentences the average length of independent clauses was 11.6 words; for declarative sentences, sorted by difficulty, the average length of independent clauses was 13.0 words (lowest difficulty), 14.3 words (medium difficulty), and 17.3 words (highest difficulty). In addition to greater syntactic complexity as indicated by number of words, the vocabulary was more difficult and thus likely to be unknown by larger numbers of students, as illustrated again by sentences from the passages on poison ivy and scarlet fever and by words like "liability," "precommitted," "chronological," "ingredients," "horse sense," and "cinema." Furthermore, in length, style, syntax, vocabulary, and topic, the "Farmer Brown," "Beat Generation," and "Suburbanites" passages are adult writing and difficult even for the seventeen year olds.

The expression "horse sense" is obviously not comprehended very widely; of the nines, thirteens, and seventeens, 64, 47, and 18 percent respectively said they would probably see the sign at "a racetrack for horses" rather than "on a highway." This is a perfect example of a multiple-choice distractor truly distracting the respondent as a result of a failure to comprehend the meaning of the question sentence. Two-thirds of the nines and half the thirteens simply didn't know "horse sense," so they selected the distractor mentioning horses and moved on to other exercises.

Inference Sentences

Tables 8 and 9 present a total of 59 sentences which not only had to be literally comprehended by the students, but also had to be confirmed as true or not true by inference from the content of given reading passages. Thus, for example, in the sentence, "The people were probably wearing coats and boots because the wind was strong and cold and the walks covered with snow," the reader may conclude that the question stem asked the student, "What were the people probably wearing?" "Coats and boots" was the correct multiple-choice response, based on the fact that the passage stated, "The wind was cold and the walks covered with snow." As with the literal-comprehension items, these three phrases and clauses were transformationally combined into the single statement the student had to process cognitively and assess for truth value. The inferential link, of course, is conveyed by the word "because." Except where otherwise noted, the theme of all items in Tables 8 and 9 is drawing inferences.

In Table 8, items at the highest correctness levels require what one might call factual inferences only, in that they unambiguously and directly follow from content given in the passages. The lower correctness levels perhaps result as much from literal-processing difficulty as from inability to perform the required inferential reasoning. Few would doubt, for example, that "Helen Keller" and the "Turtle" poem

Table 8
Inference Sentences of Lowest Difficulty
(70 to 97 percent average correctness level)

Item of Language Read and Comprehended	Percentage of Respondents Scoring Correct Answers at Each Age Level		
	Age 9	Age 13	Age 17
The object described in the verse is a flag. (untitled riddle poem)	—	—	97
The purpose of this advertisement is to get you to protect the forests. (critical reading; "Smokey Bear" poster)	—	94	98
The object described in the verse is eyeglasses. (untitled riddle poem)	—	—	96
The object described in the verse is a clock. (untitled riddle poem)	—	93	96
The author describes Helen Keller's accomplishments. ("Helen Keller")	—	—	94
The author tells us that scarlet fever may be a serious disease by telling how other infections may come with scarlet fever.	—	—	91
The fact that "assignments are not completed regularly" in algebra indicates that this student appears to have a problem in that subject. (graphic materials; reading a coded report card)	—	83	91
At least two people were in the boat. ("A Stormy Day")	86	—	—
The people were probably wearing coats and boots because the wind was strong and cold and the walks covered with snow.	84	—	—

The Reading Assessment

The person who wrote this story wanted you to laugh when you read it, because fish don't put on shoes and take long walks around the park. (critical reading)	84	—	—
Someone to rescue them could help the boy and his father now. ("A Stormy Day")	83	—	—
The mood or feeling of this story is frightening. (critical reading; "Whistling Wind")	81	84	—
The writer wants us to understand the important idea about nature that all living things are dependent on other living things. ("Farmer Brown")	—	72	93
Seeing Mt. Everest so that he could tell everyone back in Peoria that he had seen it means that he would entertain his friends back home.	—	76	83
Everything this person said can't be true because there is conflict in the ages used in the passage "for a 12-year-old," and "ever since I was 13."	—	79	—
That Silky thought flies were good playmates *best* tells how Silky felt about flies.	78	—	—
The best explanation of how the writer makes this story funny is by exaggerating the size of the flies. (critical reading)	—	75	76
The person who wrote this story was trying to tell you a funny story about a fish, because fish don't put on shoes and take long walks around the park. (critical reading)	75	—	—
That Silky's web was very big *best* tells what Silky's web was like, because he spun it from one side of the street to the other, or across the block.	75	—	—
You know this story is make-believe because ants don't give people food.	75	—	—

continued

Flies will probably not be killed by the spray, because they are not spiders, roaches, ants, or crawling insects. (written directions)	—	74	—
Tommy probably won the fight because he was only five minutes late and was happy and smiling, whereas Sammy was ten minutes late and had a black eye.	63	85	—
The fact that Christmas was only a few days away means that this story probably happened on December 21.	60	83	—
The author concludes that carefully charted debt among young couples in the United States today helps them to feel secure. ("Suburbanites")	—	55	69
Miss Sullivan's method of teaching chiefly made use of the sense of touch. (significant facts; "Helen Keller")	54	—	88
The "abyss" along which the young couples are marching is financial disaster. ("Suburbanites")	—	60	80
A turtle is speaking in this poem. (critical reading; "Turtle" poem)	56	83	—

are difficult passages for the nine year olds. "Suburbanites" and to a lesser extent "Farmer Brown" overtaxed the thirteen year olds. Perhaps only 60 percent of the nine year olds know that Christmas falls on December 25, though it seems strange that only a similar number could infer the winner of Sammy and Tommy's fight from a simple 65-word passage. An identical inference as to author's purpose had to be based on slightly different wording in the two items about the fish story. The phrase "wanted you to laugh" yielded an 84 percent correctness level at age nine, while the phrase "was trying to tell you a funny story about a fish" yielded only a 75 percent correctness level. The latter is longer and more abstractly expressed and thus assumedly more difficult to comprehend literally. This is an interesting illustration of the fact that literal comprehension rather than inferential reasoning can be the true cause of error in questions purporting to measure the ability to draw inferences.

Unmistakably, the items of language in Table 9 probed to the limits of the literal-processing and inferential-reasoning abilities of students

The Reading Assessment

Table 9
Inference Sentences of Highest Difficulty
(Below 70 percent average correctness level)

Item of Language Read and Comprehended	Percentage of Respondents Scoring Correct Answers at Each Age Level		
	Age 9	Age 13	Age 17
We know for certain that the polar ice cap can't be melting at the rate of both 3% and 7% per year. (contradictory factual claims made by two speakers in a short passage)	—	55	83
If you watched the entire movie, you could not also see the entire program about the San Diego Zoo. (reference materials; reading a TV guide)	48	72	85
Mr. Popper made Captain Cook's home in the refrigerator because penguins live in cold places. (Mr. Popper receives a penguin named Captain Cook)	67	—	—
The author's problem would have been avoided if he had arranged for accommodations well ahead of time. ("Skiing")	32	77	91
The people were probably doing last-minute shopping since Christmas was only a few days away. (shoppers in snowy cold at Christmastime)	67	—	—
The lines "I see that no one has passed here in a long time" mean that few people are searching for the truth. (from poem "The Wayfarer")	—	62	69
There is no new program listed on Channel 4 beginning at 3 p.m. because the baseball game runs until 4 p.m. (reference materials; reading a TV guide)	44	69	84
The Persian Gulf has many non-edible oysters that produce pearls.	—	60	68
It is normally true that penguins are difficult pets to care for.	63	—	—

continued

"Outstanding Sports Events of the Week" is an article you would be *most* likely to find in this magazine. (reference materials; content of magazine identified as a weekly news magazine)	—	60	65
The writer placed some of the words on the paper the way he did in order to help you see movement. (critical reading; poem "As the Cat," using unconventional typography)	62	—	—
Helen Keller lost her sight and hearing in 1882. ("Helen Keller")	40	84	—
The word "contented" best describes the speaker in the poem. (critical reading; "Turtle" poem)	—	50	72
The passage suggests that a good farmer should understand that a change in one factor of plants' surroundings may cause other factors to change. ("Farmer Brown")	—	49	70
When the writer mentions "a fine, neglected novel," he suggests that Kerouac had not received the recognition for *The Town and the City* that was deserved. ("Beat Generation")	—	48	67
The word "Wings" in Line 6 in the context of the poem means "Turns." (critical reading; poem "Auto Wreck")	29	60	78
Johnny wasn't right that he could make it rain any time he wanted to by stepping on a spider just because it rained one night after he stepped on a spider. (critical reading; claiming causality based on sequence)	—	56	—
The author's purpose in this story is to create an imaginary space story. (critical reading; "Frangibles")	35	67	—
In order to find out about an object which interested him, a Frangible would most likely enter into it. ("Frangibles")	17	59	78

The Reading Assessment

The writer used the questions at the end of the paragraph in order to help add mystery. (critical reading; "Whistling Wind")	50	—	—
The tone of the speaker is "earnest." (critical reading; passage from *Walden Two*)	—	31	56
The author's love for skiing is suggested in paragraph II. ("Skiing")	—	35	50
"Deaf heaven" refers to a God who does not hear. (critical reading; Shakespearean sonnet)	—	24	52
The word "exasperation" best describes the attitude of the speaker. (critical reading; speech from *Prometheus Bound*)	—	30	45
There was primitiveness and self-containment in Nayon before 1910 because of geographical factors. ("Village of Nayon")	—	27	45
It seems false that Earthmen were the only creatures to have traveled in space. ("Frangibles")	—	25	40
Nayon was originally separated from its neighbors because of rugged gorges traversed by rock trails. ("Village of Nayon")	—	25	29
Given the information that California bars close at 2 a.m., one may conclude that while drunk driving may be related to auto deaths, the information is inconclusive. (graphic materials; graph of auto fatalities and miles driven)	—	—	27
If you wanted to you could additionally go to the Spring Formal on Friday from 7:30 to 11:00 p.m. (graphic materials: based on a child's schedule of events for each day in the week)	—	26	—

That eating a good lunch tends to keep drivers alert to driving hazards goes

continued

beyond the data given in the chart. (graphic materials; graph of auto fatalities and miles driven)	—	17	35
By 1948 the village of Nayon was a small dependent portion of a larger economic unit. ("Village of Nayon")	—	14	23
The words "in self-entrapment is security" *best* explain the kind of human behavior described. ("Suburbanites")	—	11	26

at all three age levels. Readers may satisfy themselves by reference to Appendix A that "Frangibles," "Village of Nayon," "Suburbanites," and "Beat Generation," for example, are passages of mature and challenging writing, as are the Shakespearean sonnet and the lines from *Prometheus Bound*, "Auto Wreck," and *Walden Two*. Unfortunately, one is uncertain as to which process failed in any given item — the literal comprehension on which the inferential reasoning was contingent, or the inferencing itself, or some part of both.

The inferences from the auto-fatalities graph, of course, are based on purely graphic rather than linguistic stimuli, although the mental processes brought into play in interpreting the graph verbally, as the exercise required, are obviously language dependent. Just as obviously, however, the difficulty of the exercise lies not in the linguistic statement *per se*, but rather in correctly "seeing" the statement as necessarily implied in the graphic content. To a greater or lesser extent, this is true of questions asked about graphic materials in general.

On the three "Village of Nayon" exercises, the distribution of responses across distractors indicates that the students simply may not have known what they were doing in answering the questions. For example, the distribution on the final exercise was as follows:

	Age 13	Age 17
By 1948 the village of Nayon was		
a self-sufficient village	28	15
out of touch with the outside world	6	3
a small dependent portion of a larger economic unit (correct)	14	23
a rapidly growing and sound social and cultural unit	48	54
don't know/no response	4	5

Readers should examine the full passage in Appendix A and may hypothesize at will as to reasons explaining the distribution above. Perhaps the passage was just too difficult and/or unstimulating. Or, it might be interesting to give the above question to students without letting them see the reading passage at all and ask them to guess which answer they would pick as correct. One wonders whether the above pattern might not be duplicated by the students' semiconscious judgments about the "surface plausibility" of the distractors. In any event, the question we must ask about this exercise as well as about many others used in the assessment is, Did it measure inference, literal comprehension, willingness and perseverance, or guessing strategies?

The Rate and Comprehension Assessment

The NAEP reading assessment also measured reading rate and factual comprehension. Two passages were used at each age level, one easier than the other as indexed by a number of widely used readability formulas. Median reading rates on the six different passages were as follows:

Median Reading Rate (words per minute):	Age 9	Age 13	Age 17
Less difficult passages:	117	173	193
More difficult passages:	123	165	193

At no age did more than 10 percent of the respondents read at rates beyond 300 words per minute. Respondents were asked five recall comprehension questions on each passage. The percentages at each age who correctly answered four or five of the questions on each passage (80 to 100 percent comprehension) were the following:

Percentage of Respondents Achieving 80–100 Percent Comprehension:	Age 9	Age 13	Age 17
Less difficult passages:	73	40	67
More difficult passages:	32	35	31

Apparently either the less difficult passage or the questions asked about it were especially easy at age nine, accounting for the disproportionately high 73 percent of respondents who attained 80 percent or better comprehension.

As to rate, common sense indicates that a median reading rate of just under 200 words per minute is about the maximum one would find at any age level when respondents know that they must answer comprehension questions from memory, without returning to the reading passage. In the author's opinion, rates computed in this fashion, at least for the thirteens and seventeens, are probably lower than those at which young people ordinarily read on their own, unless of course they suffer from particular reading disabilities.

Perhaps the most interesting aspect of the foregoing results is that, although the rates for the easy and difficult passages are virtually the same at each age, the comprehension was markedly lower at all ages on the more difficult passages. This is rather clear evidence of a phenomenon all too familiar to reading and English teachers. The separate sentences (and thus the words) of a challenging passage are comprehended literally, but are not further assembled in the reader's mind as recognized components of the discourse being read. As a result, major and minor idea sequences and the development of key meanings go unrecognized, and comprehension questions cannot be answered. The reader simply fails to grasp the "idea content" of the passage. This phenomenon might be termed "sentence calling," on analogy with "word calling" among beginning readers. In word calling, individual words are read but are not understood in sentences. In sentence calling, sentences are read one at a time but are not understood in discourses. Rereading, reflection, study, discussion, and the answering of specially prepared questions continue to be the principal activities enabling students to progress from "sentence calling" to the full comprehension of discourses. Also helpful is practice in learning to adjust one's reading rate to the demands of the material being read.

Problems in Analyzing Reading Comprehension

Like most tests of reading comprehension, the National Assessment reading exercises measure word and sentence recognition as well as overt vocabulary knowledge, tacit knowledge of discourse structure, and inferential reasoning ability. The difficulty is that one cannot, short of oral testing, distinguish failures of word recognition ("decoding" in the traditional sense) from absence of word knowledge or faulty processing of syntactic or discourse structures.

For example, 35 percent of the nine year olds were unable to read and confirm the truth content of the sentence "Bubble gum that never loses its sugary flavor would stay sweet for a long time." Presumably their failure to do so stems from one or more of the following factors: inability to decode the letters b-u-b-b-l-e (or s-u-g-a-r-y, or any other) as a pronounceable English word-sound; lack of knowledge of the word-meaning (the concept) associated with each word-sound; and inability to compile the words once read into a recognized syntactic structure, or to recognize the syntactic functions of the negative of time, "never," or the conditional modal auxiliary "would." Put more generally, some reading problems result from not knowing the meanings of written words one can pronounce, others from not being able to recognize the written forms of words whose meanings and sounds one otherwise knows, and still others from an inability to recognize the syntactic features of the sentence in which they occur.

The important point is this: until these three factors are isolated and controlled in the items of a reading test or assessment, it is wrong to believe that the test or assessment is measuring awareness of higher-level features of discourse (significant facts, main ideas, organizational sequences, abstractness levels) or the ability to perform certain cognitive operations (infer purpose or tone, assess logicality, analyze humor, etc.). But the NAEP reading exercises neither provide separate information on word decoding, word knowledge, or syntactic processing, nor do they control these variables in seeking to measure discourse processing and cognitive thinking. As a result, from the point of view of someone interested in special studies of reading comprehension, the insights to be derived from the reading assessment are rather limited. It would appear from the second-round reading objectives (see Chapter Six), however, that exercises in subsequent assessments will be designed so as to overcome this problem.

Observations on Comprehension Difficulty

In looking over the exercises used in the assessment, one is struck by the vast difference in difficulty between the short reading passages written especially for the younger students and the professional writing used in exercises for older youth. As expected, this adult writing often proved difficult even for the seventeen year olds. Furthermore, there seemed to be no passages clearly identifiable as being at the medium-difficulty level. If this condition is at all true of reading material used in the schools, then it may well be the case that there exists a need in the middle school grades for more reading matter that is not quite up to the level of the "Village of Nayon" or the "Farmer Brown" passages, for example, but that challenges and exercises young readers more than do their junior novels or the artificially simplified prose of some middle-school textbooks in the content areas.

Special conventions of print format also constitute significant factors in reading. Maps, charts, forms, recipes, TV guides and so on are more difficult to read than one might think, not because their language per se is especially demanding (though it can be, as in auto insurance forms), but rather because it is broken into pieces and printed here and there in nonlinear formats. Dealing with it thus requires a series of conscious cognitive acts carried on concurrently with one's semiautomatic reading activity. For many students, especially the younger ones, such "two-variable" intellectual feats are difficult and sometimes impossible.

Note also that the syntax of written directions, recipes, and TV listings is highly elliptical, and the wording sometimes "telegraphic" in style. Communicative redundancy is thus partially reduced, and processing the language requires, at least for a time, a fair amount of conscious attention. Whenever this happens, one can be sure that failures of comprehension will increase. Language works best when we allow it to proceed spontaneously and unselfconsciously. When we are forced to attend consciously to language processing, we often experience a nearly complete shutdown of our verbal faculties. Presumably something of this sort occurred to some of the students when they encountered the special-format readings used in the assessment. The answer to the problem, one supposes, is to provide more instruction and practice in the specialized printing formats and writing conventions found in various real-life reading situations other than connected prose.

A Warning about the Reading Themes

Given the eight themes developed as reporting categories by NAEP staff members, it is natural to ask which of these themes was handled best by each of the age groups. The question can be answered, but unfortunately the answer is meaningless. To be sure, if we compute the average correctness level for the exercises in each theme, then rank the themes accordingly, we find that the nine year olds did best on words and word relationships and poorest on significant facts. The thirteens did best on directions and poorest on main ideas, and the seventeens best on directions and poorest on words and word relationships.

The reason these rankings are meaningless is that they are the result of pure happenstance. They merely indicate the average difficulty level of the exercises at each age that happened to fall into each of the thematic categories once these categories were created. Had more difficult exercises falling in the category of words and word relationships been required of the nine year olds, for example, this thematic category would have ranked lower or even lowest in average correctness level. No attempt was made to achieve a comparable mix of easy and difficult exercises in each theme, since the themes themselves were a *post hoc* invention, developed after the exercises had been given. One is therefore prevented from drawing conclusions from NAEP data as to which kinds of reading operations (which themes) students handle best or least well. Nonetheless, statements have appeared in professional literature doing just this, and should be ignored accordingly.

Judging the Reading Results

This report on the reading assessment began by stating that we should not expect the assessment results to tell us how well students are able to read. Doubtless this seemed a strange remark. For most of us, the inevitable bottom-line question that any reading assessment ought to answer is whether young people are reading as proficiently as they should be reading. Yet NAEP has quite properly refused to define "should," on the grounds that any such definition would be premature and completely arbitrary. In other words, National Assessment sets forth no standards of any kind against which to compare and judge first-round findings, in reading or in any other subject.

To understand the soundness of this policy, let us re-examine the logic of National Assessment procedures. NAEP's designers said, in effect, suppose we assemble a collection of comprehension questions based on a number of reading passages, some known to be easy and some more difficult for each age, then administer them every few years to equivalent samples of young people. The first-round results will be isolated baseline data telling us nothing. The second-round results may be higher or lower than those of round one, but will *still* not establish what measurement experts term "directionality," for the same reason that two points do not define a straight line—at least three are needed. In other words, while it may be indisputably true that the results at time B are above or below those at time A, we have no way of knowing whether it is the time-A results or the time-B results that are out of line generally.

Thus, continues NAEP reasoning, we must await the round-three assessment in order to make our first valid inferences about trends over time in the ability of young people to handle a given body of reading material. Furthermore, fourth and fifth-round results will be required to confirm or disconfirm these trends. Only then, after four or five assessments, would we be justified in treating the observed trend line as an independent standard usable in judging the results of any subsequent assessment.

If all this seems hopelessly abstract, it shouldn't. Any number of commonplace analogies come to mind. Suppose we want to ascertain trends in the annual rainfall in a certain locale. Our first year's measure is a single isolated number. The second year's measure gives us two numbers comparable only with each other, in that we don't know if it's the higher or the lower one that differs from the norm, precisely because "normal" is the very concept we're trying to establish. Only after our third measure can we expect to discern a trend, and only after two or three more can we verify this trend and claim to know what amount of rainfall is normal, and in which direction (if any) the norm is moving.

Readers should realize, of course, that the foregoing remarks are in no sense a criticism of National Assessment. Pointing a finger at the assessors for their failure to offer a normative interpretation of the first-round reading results would be as ludicrous as faulting the government for not commenting on *normal* population and growth *trends* the very first time it conducted a census.

Nor are we prevented from drawing our own individual conclusions about the correctness percentages reported on the nearly 200 reading exercises. Many of us, in fact, will agree that the recorded percentages are generally lower than we believe "should" be the case, or than we would have hoped for. Opinions of exactly this sort may be found in NAEP's *Report 02-R-30, Recipes, Wrappers, Reasoning and Rate: A Digest of the First Reading Assessment,* a concise and highly readable report written by a non-NAEP staffer, Donald R. Gallo of Central Connecticut State College. The point to remember is that subjective opinions and empirical facts are very different things. Either may be used as a basis for establishing proficiency norms, but facts usually satisfy more people and work out better over the long run.

National Assessment and Grade-Level Scores

To conclude, we may briefly turn our thoughts from assessing reading nationally to testing it in classrooms by means of commercial standardized tests. Surely *these* familiar measuring instruments, and the grade-level norms they give us, define standards of reading proficiency that should be attained by different-aged students. Surprisingly enough, they do not—although the vast majority of people who deal with them, with the exception of a seeming handful of knowledgeable reading teachers, consistently misinterpret these tests and collectively reinforce the belief that they stipulate levels of achievement ("grade level") that every child ought to attain.

First of all, the term "standardized" as used in descriptions of these tests merely means that the distribution of raw scores obtained whenever the test is given is transformed by a mathematical formula to what the statistician calls "standard-score" form. The concept has nothing to do with standards in the sense of minimum criteria or norms of desired performance.

Furthermore, the notion of "grade-level score" refers merely to the average score earned by a group of individuals in a certain grade and month in school. Suppose, for example, that a commercial test-maker develops a set of reading questions suitable for children in grades four through six. All questions are administered to a large group of students in the first month of grade four, to another in the second month of grade four, to a third group in the third month, and so on to thirty groups of students through the tenth month of grade six. For each group the average correctness score is computed. Perhaps the group in the first month of grade four average 52 correct answers, the group in the second month of grade four average 57, those in the third month 59, and so on.

Thereafter, (omitting certain details) any person scoring 52 is said to be reading at the 4.1 grade level, anyone scoring 57 is located at the 4.2 grade level, and so forth. Grade-level standards are merely the average scores achieved by students in the grade in question, on whose performance the norms were based. And obviously, the individual scores of students in any grade, including students in the groups used in establishing the test norms, are in nearly all cases either above or below this average.

The problem with standardized tests and grade-level scores is that nearly everyone treats them as if they define standards that ought to be attained by everybody. It is one thing semantically for anxious parents to hear from the reading teacher that their child is reading "below average" for his or her age, but quite another to learn that the child is "below grade level." The former is considered a natural condition of life; not everyone can be average. But the latter conjures up fears of academic failure, being kept back, and losing out in the competition for college and the good life. Denotatively, however, the two phrases "below average" and "below grade level" mean exactly the same thing when used in reference to student performance on tests of reading achievement.

This is not to suggest that parents and teachers shouldn't express concern when a child's test scores fall far below average, thus indicating the need for individual diagnosis and a program of appropriate remediation. The point is rather that when we say, as we do in so many ways, that children's reading scores should be brought "up to grade level," we are really saying "up to average," and this is a mathematical impossibility. Half the students would never catch up.

The end result of our present widespread use of year-and-month grade-level terminology is that students whose only fault is to fall below the average score of their chronologically same-aged peers are referred to as "below grade level" and are stigmatized accordingly, whereas students who score above the average are said to be "above grade level," are thought to be doing just fine, and are thus by implication licensed to rest on their laurels rather than given the motivational encouragement they too deserve. After all, a child in grade four achieving grade-five scores still cannot read at a sixth-grade level.

Another common error pertaining to year-and-month scoring terminology is that we tend to accept it at face value and assume that it denotes a real amount of time that a student is "behind" and must devote to extra study in order to "catch up," when in reality all the student need do is answer a few more questions correctly the next time he or she takes the test. Granted, this is not necessarily an easy task, but it is by no means a feat whose accomplishment requires one calendar month of extra study for each "month's worth" of test score the student is "behind."

Notice too that commercial test-makers adjust their grade-level norms annually on the basis of each year's test results and carry out full-scale renorming with new test items every few years. Thus, for example, the average ability of students in a certain grade in 1975 to read and comprehend certain material could be dramatically above or below the level achieved on comparable material by students in that grade in 1965, but because of the renorming process the phenomenon would never come to light. The average grade-level scores of both the 1965 and the 1975 students would equal their chronological grade level (i.e., they would be identical), because that is what grade-level scores are.

The National Assessment of reading, as we have seen, does not report average cumulative scores of individuals or groups, and thus its results cannot be characterized by grade-level scoring terminology. This is, in the author's view, a highly salutary fact. Because NAEP employs scoring procedures that starkly contrast with those of commercial standardized tests, the reading assessment offers us a new perspective from which to re-evaluate, and ultimately perhaps to reform, the established practices of commercial achievement testing. In the end, this could be the most important contribution of the first-round reading assessment.

Chapter Five

The Literature Assessment

Scholars have stated from time immemorial that the purpose of literature is as much to please as to edify. Some believe that literature is best defined, simply, as a particular form of pleasure, no more and no less. Hardheaded practicalists within the ranks of English teachers doubtless gauge the pragmatic value of literature as lesser than that of reading and writing and approach it primarily as a handbook for life adjustment. These persons aside, it is reasonable to suppose that the remainder of English teachers look upon the teaching of literature as the most enjoyable and best loved part of their work, the most humanizing and the most significant.

Here the unanimity ends, however, since each teacher has his or her own definition of literature and rationale for its curricular importance, including ideas about the kinds of student responses to literary works that teaching ought especially to foster. Given this diversity of viewpoints, it should not be surprising that there is little or no agreement within the profession on how best to test or assess student attainments in literary studies.

Several approaches are familiar. Objective testing ordinarily covers factual matters such as definitions of literary terms and devices, details from literary history and authors' lives, or the factual content of literary works—characters' names, aspects of plot and setting, and so on. Tests of critical ability such as the Advanced Placement examinations of the College Board require students to write exegetical essays interpreting and evaluating literary selections not previously read or studied. No particular critical approach is required, although the close-reading techniques of old-fashioned "New Criticism" continue to predominate. British university examinations require mastery of the factual material just mentioned plus the memorization of large amounts of critical commentary on a canon of longer works intensively studied in class.

Each form of testing in literature has its advocates and vocal opponents. Moreover, not a few English teachers hold that all forms of testing are alien to the spirit of literature and pervert its essential purpose. Within this milieu of disagreement, both friendly and hostile, the first National Assessment of literature took shape. In the author's view, the literature assessment was planned as a first step only in its intended direction — cautious, conservative, almost tentative, and frankly experimental in places. Clearly it was designed to rankle as few people as possible. What readers must now ask themselves, in examining the literature assessment, is the extent to which, in seeking to remain innocuous, it nonetheless succeeded in achieving a sufficiently high level of significance.

The Literature Objectives and Exercises

The objectives and exercises for the literature assessment were developed by the Educational Testing Service following procedures identical to those used in the writing assessment. The three objectives were as follows:

1. Read literature of excellence:
    a. be acquainted with a wide variety of literary works,
    b. understand the basic metaphors and themes through which man has expressed his values and tensions in Western culture.
2. Become engaged in, find meanings in, and evaluate a work of literature:
    a. respond to a work of literature,
    b. find meanings in a work of literature, and read a work with literary comprehension,
    c. evaluate a work of literature.
3. Develop a continuing interest and participation in literature and the literary experience:
    a. be intellectually oriented to literature,
    b. be affectively oriented to literature,
    c. be independently active and curious about literature,
    d. relate literary experience to one's life.

Here again, readers may wish to look ahead to Chapter Six and compare the revised literature objectives, to be used in future assessments, with the foregoing list.

A variety of exercise items were constructed to measure the attainment of these objectives. One set of exercises sought to examine knowledge of specific literary works and characters. Another group of exercises measured the ability to process literary language and understand features of form, metaphor, implied meaning, and tone. A third group presented the students with short poems or stories and asked that they respond to each work in some way, either by defending their multiple-choice answer to a given question, or by making open-ended comments in written essays, or by orally answering a three-part question sequence. The fourth and final set of exercises asked about reading habits, attitudes, and experiences.

In a manner similar to that of the reading assessment, NAEP staff writers invented four thematic categories to which the literature exercises were assigned for reporting purposes. The theme names are reflected in the titles of the four primary literature reports published by NAEP:

> Theme One: Report 02-L-01, Understanding Imaginative Literature
> Theme Two: Report 02-L-02, Responding to Literature
> Theme Three: Report 02-L-03, Recognizing Literary Works and Characters
> Theme Four: Report 02-L-04, A Survey of Reading Habits

Knowledge of Literary Works

Table 10 indicates the percentage of students at each age level who were able to recognize specific literary works and characters. The items identified as parodies, allusions, or stories parallel to the work in question were in multiple-choice format. Items showing a picture of a literary character were fill-in-the-blank completion questions. The final items asked "Have you heard of?" and required a "yes" or "no" response plus minimal corroborative information. (Note: Remember that a horizontal line indicates that the exercise was not administered to the age in question.)

Looking at these percentages, one notes the generally high totals on most items at most ages. Indeed, many of the characters and works included are in a sense literary cliches. Knowing something about them is probably more a matter of common knowledge than proof that the respondent has actually read all or parts of the piece of literature in question. Exceptions to the rule of widespread knowledge are Don Quixote, Job, Thor, and ogres. One may interpret these facts as one wishes.

Had the assessors attempted to measure knowledge of less familiar titles and characters, albeit ones found even in a majority of school literature programs (Henry Fleming, Jay Gatsby, or Holden Caulfield, for example), they would have been open to the charge of assuming a nationwide literature curriculum that does not in fact exist, and thus of discriminating against those students whose schools happened not to teach the works in question. The alternative apparently pursued by NAEP was to ask about information assumed ahead of time to be known by practically everyone. *Charlotte's Web* may have been the one surprise.

Understanding Literary Language

Exercises in this category were of four different kinds. Each type is described and shown separately in Table 11. The missing-line and metaphor exercises were in multiple-choice format, and percentages are shown for each distractor as well as for the correct answers.

Table 10
Percentage of Respondents Recognizing
Specific Literary Works and Characters

Literary Work or Character	Age 9	Age 13	Age 17
Pictures of:			
Little Red Riding Hood	86	94	—
Moby Dick	—	—	87
Little Bo Peep	71	—	—
Tortoise and the Hare	52	70	81
Sherlock Holmes	—	57	79
Alice in Wonderland	45	72	74
Winnie the Pooh	48	58	54
Charlotte's Web	33	36	—
Don Quixote	—	8	21
Parodies of:			
Casey at the Bat	37	76	87
The Village Blacksmith	—	42	60
The Charge of the Light Brigade	—	—	49
Allusions to:			
Tom Sawyer	—	91	93
Noah	—	88	93
Samson	—	85	93
Adam	—	67	80
Venus	—	—	64
David	—	—	54
Galahad	—	41	61
Parallel Story Patterns:			
The Trojan Horse	—	68	81
Job	—	15	36
Have You Ever Heard of? ("yes" responses)			
Daniel Boone	93	—	—
The Ugly Duckling	89	—	—
Rumpelstiltskin	76	—	—
Paul Bunyan	57	—	—
Cupid	50	—	—
an ogre	25	—	—
Thor	17	—	—

The Literature Assessment

Table 11
Percentage of Responses to Objective Items
Measuring Understanding of Literary Language

Exercise Item	Age 9	Age 13	Age 17

1. Missing-Line Exercise. Three short poems were presented with one or two lines omitted. Respondents then identified the omitted line from a multiple-choice listing.

First Snow
Snow makes whiteness where it falls,
The bushes look like popcorn-balls.
and places where I always play,

(right) Look like somewhere else today.	40	56	—
(wrong) Look at me when I come to stay.	15	8	—
(wrong) Look just the same as yesterday.	42	34	—

There was an old man with a beard
Who said, "It is just what I feared!
   Two owls and a hen
   Four larks and a wren

(right) Have all built their nests in my beard!"	49	68	80
(wrong) Are in my beard."	24	17	11
(wrong) Are flying around and around my nice beard!"	23	14	7

The airplane taxis down the field
And heads into the breeze,
It lifts its wheels above the ground,
It skims above the trees,

It's just a speck against the sky
— and now it's gone!

(right) It rises high and higher Away up toward the sun	—	83	92
(wrong) It dips and lands again Its journey now is done	—	10	5
(wrong) I'd like to be a pilot I know it would be fun	—	6	2

continued

2. Pun Exercises. Respondents were told the meaning of "pun" and were then asked to identify the pun, if one was present, in three statements.

The only way to double your money is to fold it and put it into your pocket.	21	44	—
You've got a very good nose as noses run.	—	—	48
Always spread newspapers out in front of the fireplace so if any sparks fly out they won't get on the rug. (not a pun)	48	67	54

3. Metaphors. Respondents were given three short pieces of verse and one prose sentence containing metaphors, then were asked to identify first the literal comparison, then the intention, of the metaphor.

Hope is a thing with feathers
That perches in the soul,
And sings the tune without the words,
And never stops at all.

Hope is made to be like			
(right) a bird	47	—	88
(wrong) the soul	41	—	11
(wrong) an Indian	6	—	1
Hope is meant to be			
(right) cheerful and dependable	76	—	86
(wrong) silent and shy	10	—	11
(wrong) irregular and sad	7	—	2

The fog comes
on little cat feet.
It sits looking
over harbor and city
on silent haunches
and then moves on.

The cat's feet are compared to			
(right) slow moving mist	63	82	85
(wrong) the rain	12	3	3
(wrong) the tops of buildings	17	12	10
The fog is meant to be seen as			
(right) quiet and stealthy	70	80	90
(wrong) loud and clumsy	11	4	2
(wrong) majestic and proud	12	14	7

The Literature Assessment

There is something in October sets the gypsy
    blood astir;
We must rise and follow her,
When from every hill of flame
She calls and calls each vagabond by name.

"Hill of flame" describes			
(right) autumn trees	—	61	—
(wrong) gypsies	—	15	—
(wrong) fire	—	21	—
The author meant by "hill of flame"			
(right) brightly colored trees	—	60	—
(wrong) gypsies' campfire	—	30	—
(wrong) October sunshine	—	8	—

Slang is language that takes off its coat, spits on its hands, and gets to work.

"Takes off . . . to work" describes			
(right) an honest laborer	—	69	85
(wrong) a foreigner	—	8	3
(wrong) a criminal	—	20	8
The writer of this sentence *probably*			
(right) liked slang	—	56	68
(wrong) never used slang	—	10	9
(wrong) thought slang should never be used	—	26	15

4. Similarity of Form Exercises. Respondents were given four short excerpts from works of literature and were told to identify "the two that are alike in the way they are written." They were then asked to select from a list the term characterizing the likeness. Percentages of respondents who correctly performed these tasks follow.

Recognized two verse passages as distinct from passages of prose and drama	71	84	91
Recognized the two as "poems"	62	79	85
Recognized two first-person prose passages as distinct from passages of drama and third-person prose	—	58	—
Recognized the two as "first person narrative"	—	27	—

continued

Recognized a stage direction and passage of dialogue as distinct from passages of verse and prose:	—	—	18
Recognized the two as "plays"	—	—	17

On first inspection, the responses reported in Table 11 appear to constitute quite well-behaved data. In all cases but one (the final pun item) where an exercise was given to more than a single age group, older students outperformed younger ones, as we would expect. Only a little over half of the nine year olds are consistently able to deal adequately with literary language. The percentage of correct responses was quite high for the seventeen year olds, however, on all except the pun items and the final similarity-of-form item, which are flawed in a manner explained below. These high standings indicate that students completing their high school years have attained general proficiency in processing the language of literature. We should expect no more from the nine year olds, and no less from the seventeens.

The pun exercises caused trouble for all ages, but the difficulty presumably arose from exercise format rather than content. Respondents were instructed to underline the pun in each statement containing one and were scored unacceptable if they underlined too much or too little. But NAEP does not report exactly which words were to be underlined. In the "noses run" sentence, given at all three age levels, we learn that in addition to the correct responses reported, another 39, 27, and 46 percent respectively recognized full well that the sentence contained a pun, but underlined the wrong word(s). Presumably the correct words were "noses run" and "run" alone was incorrect. But is it? How many teachers would wish to defend this hair-splitting decision to students outraged by the fact that they knew perfectly well a pun was present and what it was, but were tripped up by a scoring punctilio?

In a similar vein, the seventeens were totally confused by the final similarity-of-form item, in which a paragraph-length stage direction from Shaw's *Caesar and Cleopatra* had to be likened to four lines of dialogue from Albee's *The American Dream*. Nothing in the stage direction clearly identified it as such. Since form was the matter at issue, rather than knowledge of particular works, a strong case could be made for interpreting the stage direction as a piece of present-tense prose narrative, which in form it was. And in fact, 51 percent of the seventeens did just this, likening it to a distractor that was also in narrative-prose form. In short, the exercise was badly made.

Assessment Questions versus Teaching Questions

Overall, the more one examines the items in Table 11 the more one is drawn towards two conclusions applicable to the classroom. First, one is forced to consider the contribution that exercises of this sort, given as classroom practice activities, may make towards increasing students' knowledge of the workings of literary language. Notice that each of these exercises causes the student to attend consciously to a particular aspect or part of a work of literature that might otherwise be passed over, often by means of considering what the effect on the work would be had alternative language been employed instead of the word or line the writer actually used. For the many teachers who understand the phrase "teaching literature" to mean illustrating how literature may be fully read by drawing readers' attention to the "workings" of particular works, querying students in the manner of the Table 11 exercises constitutes the essential teaching act.

In light of this, the second conclusion arising from consideration of these exercises stresses the importance, in everyday teaching, of asking valid questions couched in valid formats and having valid answers. Here we may learn from both the strengths and the weaknesses of Table 11 exercises. Consider the first missing-line item, on the poem "First Snow." The jingling iambic rhythm of "Look just the same as yesterday" entrapped 42 percent of the nine year olds and 34 percent of the thirteen year olds, who heard but presumably didn't think about the content of the line. What an excellent teaching moment this would be in the classroom—an opportunity to draw to students' attention not only the fact that "bushes" looking like some*thing* quite different in our imagination (popcorn balls) constitutes the first half of an idea pattern later repeated when "places where I always play" look like some*where* else, but also that the trochaic rhythm of the first line is repeated in that of the last, "Look like somewhere else today," such that the poem comes full circle, inviting beholders of snow to make their own metaphors reimagining the familiar. In microcosm so minute as to seem trivial, this exercise as a potential instrument of instruction exemplifies exactly what literature teaching should contain and aim to accomplish.

But the items in Table 11 also illustrate the pitfalls awaiting one in preparing materials for this sort of teaching. In the metaphor exercises, for example in Emily Dickinson's "Hope" poem, one notes the difficulty of finding suitable distractors for multiple choice questions. In the "Hope is meant to be" question, "silent and shy" and "irregular and sad" are so obviously wrong that 76 percent of the nine year olds guessed that "cheerful and dependable" was correct, although only 47 percent had recognized that the content of the metaphor was the comparison of hope to a bird. On the other hand, if distractors are used that are only a little wrong, "energetic and persistent" for instance, then they are also partly right and can't in fairness be scored unacceptable. Where the item is used in a teaching situation, of course, partially true answers may be discussed and often form the basis of fuller teaching. The trouble occurs where partially true distractors occur in test exercises, where they must be scored right or wrong.

Other problems are similarly exemplified in the metaphor items. In Sandburg's "Fog," the content question is asked wrong-end-around. The poem does not compare a cat or cat's feet to fog; it compares fog to a cat. In the Bliss Carmen poem, the literal object of comparison (trees) is unstated, so the content question had to be "What does 'hill of flames' describe?" rather than 'What are trees made to be like?" As a consequence, there was no way of phrasing the intention question such that "trees" modified in some way ("brightly colored") was not a part of the correct response. Not only did this give away the answer to the content question, it in effect merely asked the same question over again—a fact confirmed by the 61 and 60 percent correctness levels attained by respondents. The "slang" questions are phrased clearly enough. The trouble here is that, for younger students, the term "slang" itself is so loaded with negative connotations that one-fourth of the thirteen year olds checked the third distractor, "slang should never be used," probably more as reflex behavior than as considered action.

In any event, the general interpretation arising from a consideration of Table 11 items is that exercises requiring close attention to literary language should not be regarded as testing devices alone. Rather they are teaching instruments par excellence. Used for either purpose they are assessment questions in form, but in the classroom they are the very questions by means of which we teach. Thus it is crucial that they be well formulated. By paying careful attention to the weaknesses and strengths of the questions asked in the literature assessment, we can improve the quality of similar questions used in our teaching.

Assessing Response to Literature

Almost fifty years ago, as a result of experiments reported in his widely-read volume *Practical Criticism*, the critic and teacher I. A. Richards concluded that an educated reader's sequence of response to a literary work progresses from literal comprehension—which for Richards meant grasping "the plain sense of the text"—to apprehension first of its figurative language, then of its tonal qualities, and finally of its full intention. Since the pioneering work of Richards, no topic has so constantly excited the curiosity of researchers in the teaching of literature as that inherent in the apparently simple questions: What happens when one reads a work of literature? How are one's responses to be described and accounted for? Thus it was only natural that National Assessment would seek information on response to literature.

But there are great difficulties in researching this topic. Foremost of these is the fact that the primary data of response remain unconscious in the mind of the reader. What is accessible to introspection is a confused jumble, only fragments of which can ever be externalized verbally. And even if introspective data or "inner speech" could be gotten out and recorded, they would constitute but the tip of an iceberg with respect to the unconscious conceptual and judgmental processing performed by the mind whenever any verbal discourse is received, whether or not it is literary in form.

Other practical research problems also appear. Multiple-choice questions force the reader to select the best of another's responses to the work in question rather than one's own. Open-ended essay questions allow full freedom for the expression of response, but impose the additional burden that the persons answering must compose their responses in some organized fashion. Broadly speaking, they must in effect produce one literary work in response to another literary work, and in so doing must strike off from the original work in any one of an indefinite number of possible directions, more or less ignoring all the others. Furthermore, writing about literary works constitutes a particular kind of rhetorical task, and students ordinarily require special instruction in order to perform it.

A middle course would be to follow up multiple-choice questions by requiring respondents to justify their answers, or to pose channeling questions which would direct verbally composed responses into one or another of the large categories into which such responses typically fall (see below). National Assessment used both these approaches plus open-ended response questions in what was clearly an experimental manner. Exercise types were the following:

1. multiple-choice questions, with the added feature that the respondents were required to give reasons in their own words justifying their choices;
2. orally composed and tape-recorded answers to three open-ended channeling questions asked about given works of literature;
3. essays written in answer to a single question asked about a given work, in effect, what do you have to say about this poem or story?

The question of meaningfully characterizing the various responses also bedeviled the assessors. It was decided that two readers would rate each oral or written response on a four-point adequacy scale: inadequate, barely adequate, adequate, and superior. Readers who examine *Report 02-L-02, Responding to Literature* will find therein brief instructions to the readers characterizing each adequacy level, as well as samples of the oral and written responses elicited by the different exercises.

In addition to adequacy judgments, it was also decided that each response would be sorted into one or another of the four major categories of the Purves-Rippere literary-response taxonomy.* This is an exhaustive category scheme for classifying any conceivable statement made about a work of literature. But problems with the Purves-Rippere taxonomy are twofold. For one thing, like any taxonomy unrelated to a systematic theory, the classification is arbitrary and gives no insight into the processes of literary response, only their apparent products. For another, using the taxonomy is extremely time consuming, since each T-unit (independent clause) in a reader's response must be separately analyzed and classified. (Indeed, it is clear that the analysis must penetrate to each embedded sentence in any T-unit, and no researcher as yet has published the results of such an analysis.) In the end, National Assessment settled for the holistic classification of complete essays, not into the terminal categories of the Purves-Rippere taxonomy, but rather into its four general categories:

1. Engagement-Involvement: What effect does the work have on the reader as an individual?
2. Perception: What are the literal, formal, figural, and tonal features of the work?
3. Interpretation: What does the work mean? What is its intention in regard to the world outside itself?
4. Evaluation: Is the work of art a good work of art?

Responses not classifiable in the foregoing categories were identified as "retelling and paraphrase," "unusual" (total irrelevancies), and "unclassifiable" (containing equal amounts of content belonging to two or more categories). Altogether, nine pieces of literature were used in the personal response items, six poems and three short stories. The poems are given in Appendix B, but the short stories are identified by bibliographical reference only.

Multiple-Choice-plus-Reasons Response Exercises

First of all, three multiple-choice questions were asked requiring written statements of reasons in support of the answer chosen. Results are shown in Table 12.

Here one notices the difference between the ability to select a correct multiple-choice answer provided by the test maker and the ability to say in at least a "barely adequate" fashion why this answer is correct in terms of the given piece of literature. Most nine year olds, incidentally, are too young to write reasoned argumentation and probably should not have been asked to do so. In both instances, only half of the thirteens who identified the correct multiple-choice answer

---

*Alan C. Purves with Victoria Rippere. Elements of Writing about a Literary Work. Urbana, Illinois: National Council of Teachers of English, 1968.

Table 12
Percentage of Responses to Multiple-Choice Questions
Requiring Written Statement of Supporting Reasons

Exercise Item	Age 9	Age 13	Age 17
In the poem "As the Cat," the poet is really			
(right) describing the cat's movements	78	95	—
adequate supporting reasons given	14	54	—
(wrong) worried about the cat	7	2	—
(wrong) being mad at the cat	6	1	—
(wrong) being sad about the cat	3	17	—
In the poem "The Closing of the Rodeo," the mood is			
(right) sad	—	83	86
adequate supporting reasons given	—	41	64
(wrong) angry	—	4	5
(wrong) cheerful	—	5	4
(wrong) humorous	—	7	2
In the poem "Sport," the poet is really			
(right) being angry at hunters	—	—	50
adequate supporting reasons given	—	—	40
(wrong) cheering the hunters on	—	—	6
(wrong) feeling sorry for animals	—	—	20
(wrong) just describing hunters and animals	—	—	21

could adequately support their choices, even though the latter were fairly obvious. Among the seventeens, however, approximately four out of five were able to explain their choices adequately. These results may be functions of increased knowledge about literature, improved ability to compose written language, or both. In any case, the two factors are confounded in the Table 12 exercises.

The exercise on the "Sport" poem merits further consideration, since it constitutes yet another example of the problems inherent in attempting to measure interpretations of literature using a multiple-choice format. Clearly, the question stem in this item places far too great a weight on the word "really" and includes two distractors in addition to the correct response for which arguments can be made. The literalist will never be persuaded that the poet is doing more than "just describing hunters and animals." A distractor offering this form of escape from the problems of identifying tone should never be included. Further, for many readers, the poet is just as much "feeling sorry for animals" as "being angry at hunters"; indeed, they would argue that the anger stems from the sorrow. The problem here is that numerous correct interpretations are assignable to many literary works, a fact we constantly need to remember in our classroom teaching. What is most important, of course, is not so much *which* interpretation students put forward as *how* they support the positions they choose by critical readings of the text in question.

Everything considered, however, the assessment technique of requiring respondents to defend in their own words a multiple-choice interpretative answer is potentially quite good. Notice the strategy involved. One selects ahead of time a certain perception or interpretation of a work. This is then embedded in a set of multiple-choice distractors, so that one need not trust to chance in hoping for its appearance, as is the case with open-ended response questions. The crux of the matter, and the source of interest, is how well and in what terms the respondent defends (in effect, explicates) the perception or interpretation which he believes, through the ruse of the multiple-choice selection, to be his own. This method of assessing the ability to respond to works of literature with insight and comprehension surely deserves wider use, since its claims on validity run higher than those of either multiple-choice or open-ended questions used separately, and it may contribute to the development of writing skills and the heightening of student interest and involvement.

Channeling-Questions-plus-Oral-Answers Response Exercises

Turning to the oral answers to questions about certain works, the three channeling questions asked of all respondents were:

1. Tell me what you most want to say about the story or poem. (Designed to elicit an engagement-involvement response.)
2. What did you especially notice in the story or poem? (Designed to elicit a perceptive or interpretative response.)
3. Tell me what you think about the story. (Designed to elicit an evaluative response.)

The entire answer given by a respondent to each channeling question was, where possible, assigned to one of the four general response categories. Many of the answers were not assignable to any of the categories. Table 13 reports the percentage of oral statements that were judged "barely adequate" or better after being assigned to a response category. Because of the manner in which NAEP reported the scores, it is not possible to determine what percentage of the total of all statements (three per respondent) was assigned to each category, although this would have been interesting information, since students of different ages perhaps favor one type of response to others, regardless of the channeling questions they may be asked.

Perhaps the most surprising information in Table 13 is the similarity of totals between ages thirteen and seventeen in the adequacy

Table 13
Percentages of Oral Responses Judged Adequate
In Each of Four Major Response Categories

Literary Selection	Age 9	Age 13	Age 17
"Sam, Bangs and Moonshine" (short story)			
Engagement	45	—	—
Perception	1	—	—
Interpretation	27	—	—
Evaluation	6	—	—
"If Apples Were Pears" (poem)			
Engagement	42	—	—
Perception	27	—	—
Interpretation	16	—	—
Evaluation	4	—	—
"Space Travellers" (poem)			
Engagement	45	45	—
Perception	14	28	—
Interpretation	7	24	—
Evaluation	6	7	—
"The Closing of the Rodeo" (poem)			
Engagement	—	35	32
Perception	—	21	21
Interpretation	—	41	50
Evaluation	—	7	8

levels of statements made on the "Rodeo" poem. Although we do not know how many of the respondents at either age level favored one kind of response over the others, it is clear that statement for statement, the thirteens reached "barely adequate" or higher levels just as often as did the seventeens, although the standards for judging adequacy may well have been different for each age. On the face of it, however, the thirteens are as able as the seventeens in responding insightfully to this rather simple poem. The fact that more engagement-involvement statements were adequate than were those in the other categories may or may not be significant. The relative difficulty of statements of the four major kinds has never been independently measured, but it would seem that those expressing mere engagement with a work would indeed be least difficult. In fact, it is hard to imagine how the notion of "adequacy" can even come into play with respect to engagement-involvement statements.

Written-Essay Response Exercises

Finally, the thirteens and seventeens were requested to write essay

Table 14
Percentage of Total and Adequate Written Responses
Classified According to Five Response Categories

Literary Selection	Age 13 Total	Age 13 Adequate	Age 17 Total	Age 17 Adequate
"Space Travellers" (poem)				
Engagement	9	9	—	—
Perception	3	3	—	—
Interpretation	29	28	—	—
Evaluation	9	7	—	—
Retelling	33	17	—	—
"Into My Heart" (poem)				
Engagement	—	—	3	2
Perception	—	—	1	1
Interpretation	—	—	86	86
Evaluation	—	—	1	1
Retelling	—	—	1	1
"Half a Gift" (short story)				
Engagement	12	12	—	—
Perception	0	0	—	—
Interpretation	21	20	—	—
Evaluation	4	3	—	—
Retelling	55	33	—	—
"Snake Dance" (short story)				
Engagement	—	—	9	9
Perception	—	—	1	1
Interpretation	—	—	56	56
Evaluation	—	—	5	5
Retelling	—	—	25	23

answers in response to the following directive: "Write a composition in which you discuss the poem or story. We are more interested in what you have to say than in how well you say it." Each essay as a whole was assigned to the response category to which its content predominantly belonged. The essays were then rated for adequacy as described above. Table 14 reports information on these essay responses. A fifth category has been added, "retelling," to indicate essays in which the writer merely restated or paraphrased the content of the work. Since each respondent wrote only one essay, which was assigned to one category only, it is possible to see (under the "Total" headings) the extent to which each category of response was favored by each age group. Percentages under the "Adequate" headings indicate the number of essays in each category judged minimally adequate or better. Failure of reported percentages to total 100 results from the fact that some essays were considered anomalous on various grounds and could not be placed in the given categories.

Table 14 appears to reflect criteria for deciding minimal adequacy quite different from those used in the oral-statement exercises reported in Table 13. Here virtually all the essays were judged "barely adequate" or higher, except those on the short stories in the retelling category. Contrast these results with the very low adequacy totals reported in Table 13. Unfortunately, National Assessment provides no information about different criteria that may have been utilized in the adequacy ratings. Thus it is impossible to reach conclusions about student abilities in different response modes—oral answers to channeling questions versus essays written on open-ended topics.

Table 14 does indicate a shift of preferred response category between ages thirteen and seventeen. With the poems, practically all the retelling responses disappear, and the number of interpretive responses increases by nearly threefold. With the short stories, retelling is halved and interpretation doubled. This is a rather dramatic change, undergone during the high school years. Presumably it is the result of English instruction, although we cannot know this for certain. Nor can we tell whether the interpretive response mode constitutes the true preference of the seventeens, or merely the category they have been conditioned to choose when put to the test, so to speak, in school writing tasks not unlike that of the NAEP exercises. One is tempted to conclude that experiences in high school English do play a part in this shift of response category. Whether the shift is actual or only apparent, however, and whether if actual it is desirable or undesirable educationally, are questions one must go beyond the assessment data to answer.

Survey of Reading Habits and Attitudes

The final section of the literature assessment surveyed attitudes and the prior reading experience of students in the three age groups. It is important to note that the assessors asked respondents to name titles of works they claimed to have read and verified each as the actual title of an existing work. Some respondents were able to name as many as four or five or even more. Table 15 reports the percentages of "yes" responses to questions pertaining to in-school as well as out-of-school reading.

Both the question list and the literary genres mentioned in Table 15 are ranked from highest to lowest average percentage at each age level. The extremely high percentages of thirteens and seventeens who believe literature an important and valuable subject of study should be most heartening to middle and high school English teachers. The second question indicates that young people fully accept the cinema as an authentic medium of literary experience along with

Table 15
Percentage of "Yes" Responses to Questions
About Literary Reading Habits and Attitudes

Question Asked	Age 9	Age 13	Age 17
Do you believe it is important to study literature in school?	—	77	90
Do you think movies should be studied as part of English classes?	—	—	84
Do you think reading great literature is of any value?	—	—	79
Have you ever seen a play, movie, or TV version of a book you have read?	—	65	77
Have you ever read a work of literature a second time?	—	56	57
Have you ever read more than one book by the same author?	—	46	51
Have you ever read a version of a play, movie, or TV show you have seen?	—	41	41
Can you give the title of one or more works of the following kinds of literature that you have read during the past year? [In addition to "yes," names of one or more verifiable titles were required.]			
Books of poems	—	66	65
Novels	—	54	70
Biographies	—	56	43
Plays	—	32	43
Books of short stories	—	17	20
Do you sometimes-to-often like to read the following?			
Fiction	93	93	—
Nonfiction	89	89	—
Poems	85	73	—
Stories about America	88	—	—
Stories about other lands	85	—	—
Short stories	—	92	—
News Magazines	—	86	—
Plays	—	57	—
Editorials	—	51	—
Reviews of literature	—	34	—

Table 16
Percentage of "Yes" Responses to Questions
about Voluntary Out-of-School Reading Habits

Question Asked	Age 9	Age 13	Age 17
Do you read for your own enjoyment during your spare time at least once a week or more?	84	77	—
Can you give the title of one or more works of the following kinds of literature that you have read on your own outside of school? [In addition to "yes," names of one or more verifiable titles were required.]			
Novels	65	54	69
Biographies	36	55	52
Poems	33	24	25
Magazines	46	—	—
Short stories	—	38	36
Plays	—	22	33
Epic Poems	—	21	23
Essays	—	4	14
Literary criticism	—	1	5

live-stage and print. But who any longer regards this fact as either surprising or lamentable? What does strike one here is the overall evidence that literature has by no means died out as an art mode, despite premature reports of its demise. Note too that poetry is the genre remembered by the highest percentage of thirteens and the second highest of the seventeens as having been read during the year preceding. One hopes, of course, that the recollection is fond. Novels enjoy a large increase in readership during the high-school years, perhaps being well remembered for the protracted in-class study they so frequently occasion.

The questions reported in Table 16 asked about voluntary out-of-school reading only, and thus enable us to examine preferences apart from school requirements—assuming, of course, that the students were able to separate the two in memory, and were truthful. If so, a comparison of the percentages in Tables 15 and 16 on novels read indicates that remembered books are not school-assigned material after all, but rather the novels students read on their own, since the figures are identical in the two tables. Not so with poetry, where over half of that read appears to have been required in school. The decline in the reading of biography from thirteen to seventeen, reflected in both tables, is consistent with Erik Erikson's "stages of man" theory, wherein earlier problems of role identification and identity, which prompt the reading of biography, give way to the search for intimacy and the meaning of existence, which form the themes of quality prose fiction.

The thirteens and seventeens who said they believed literature an important subject for schools to teach (77 and 90 percent respectively) were asked to give reasons for their beliefs. The following categories emerged:

Reasons for Teaching Literature	Age 13	Age 17
1. Literature improves language skills and helps one in English:	25	15
2. Literature is important for one's future education or job:	11	6
3. Literature increases awareness of other people's opinions:	2	11
4. Literature gives one various other kinds of knowledge:	3	12
5. Literature teaching increases one's understanding of literature:	5	2
6. Other acceptable reasons:	2	6
7. Literature has no value and/or is not enjoyable:	7	4
8. Didn't know or didn't respond:	9	2
9. Empty, uninterpretable, and non-applicable responses:	36	42

Traditionally, of course, laymen and literary critics alike have been allowed to put forth whatever reasons they wished to justify the study of literature. Categories one and two, however, reflect the kind of unreasoned pragmatic value that "good" students, when asked, automatically impute to all their school subjects. One notes with satisfaction that percentages of these responses decline with age. Categories three through six, covering what most teachers would consider the range of desirable responses, total 12 and 13 percent respectively for the two ages. The increase is encouraging to be sure, yet the sobering fact remains that only one-third of the 90 percent of high school seniors who believe literature an important subject of study can advance as much as one clear and sensible reason for their belief.

Clearly we should encourage student discussions on the value of literature ranging beyond the typical perfunctory comments about its

The Literature Assessment

real-world pragmatic value. In a fundamental way, literature is language at play, to be written and read purely for the fun of it. As teachers we tend to forget this fact, and we ought to allow students more of an opportunity to verbalize it on their own, since their intuitions are very likely fresher and nearer the surface than our own and deserve to be kept that way.

Finally, the assessors categorized the verified book titles students said they had read and ranked the categories according to the number of works contained in each. The top three categories for each age are as follows:

Age 9

1. fairy tales and other fantasy;
2. children's and teen's activities and adventures (e.g., Nancy Drew and Hardy Boys books, *Heidi*, *Little Women*, Curious George, Happy Hollisters and Betsy series, etc.);
3. other children's books (these tell stories, but not enough was known about them to enable further categorization).

Age 13

1. children's books (books in this category are listed in the Wilson *Children's Catalogue* as juvenile or elementary school reading: White's *Charlotte's Web* and *Stuart Little*, books by Laura Ingalls Wilder, etc.);
2. young people's general reading (these are novels and long stories listed in the Wilson catalogues for senior and junior high school libraries and shelved in the public libraries as fiction for grades 7–12; popular in this category were Hardy Boys and Nancy Drew mysteries, sports stories for teenagers, horse and dog novels, nurse books, romances, and old standbys like *Old Yeller*, *Johnny Tremain*, *The Outsiders*, etc.);
3. popular fiction (past and present bestsellers, all novels reviewed in major book reviewing periodicals and appearing in *Book Review Digest*, but not candidates for "classic" status).

Age 17

1. popular fiction of literary merit (the novels in this category are not old enough to be considered "classics," yet they are not just "popular fiction" either, and are taught regularly in college literature classes);
2. popular fiction (defined above in Age 13);
3. adult classics (the novels in this category are enduring works of fiction taught in college literature courses as classics and published in various classics series; for a basic reference, scorers used the E. P. Dutton "Everyman's Library," Standard Edition Title Index).

Mental maturation and the progressive development of interests and tastes are reflected in the foregoing results, which corroborate existing surveys of different-aged reading interests. National Assessment has published additional information on specific titles of literary works read by students (Report 02-L-04, A Survey of Reading Habits), but has neither compiled the full listing of works mentioned nor constructed a popularity ranking based on the number of mentions received by each. Many teachers would find a ranked list of this sort quite valuable, expecially if it were to appear immediately after the information was collected.

Interpreting the Literature Assessment

Taken as a whole, the literature assessment yielded information on students' knowledge of literary works and characters, their ability to comprehend features of literary language, and their reading habits and attitudes towards literature. The assessment also generated a body of oral and written prose responses to given literary works.

The exercises assessing knowledge of individual works failed to include selections from even the most familiar English and American literature typically read in the upper secondary grades. Obviously there are many hundreds of works to choose from, and a given assessment has room for only a few. No matter what choices are made, they will inevitably discriminate against respondents whose English programs happen not to include the works chosen. If the assessing of individual works were to be announced in advance or repeated in subsequent assessment cycles, talk would be heard of a "National Assessment Literature List." NAEP does not want this, nor do teachers. Furthermore, the number of students who have heard of a given work or character is certainly much larger than the number who have actually read the work. Nor in the end is it very important to have either kind of information. All things considered, assessment time in future rounds might better be spent on exercises other than ones measuring knowledge of literary works and characters.

The survey of habits and attitudes yielded information that should restore optimism to all literature teachers. Young people are reading on their own, reading quite widely, and reading more mature and demanding works the older they become. Television has not killed the reading habit, and English teachers after all are more than merely curators of an endangered species. Although the ritual chorus "We hate poetry!" will doubtless continue to resound in the middle secondary grades, the NAEP survey clearly indicates that poetry is not in fact the disliked genre students pretend it is.

Perhaps the response-to-literature exercises produced the most disappointing results of the entire literature assessment, in that so little can be interpreted from the numerical information reported. We are not especially interested in knowing the percentage of students who have spoken or written a purportedly adequate response to a poem or short story unless we first learn what the response task and the adequacy criteria were, then can satisfy ourselves that these were sharply focused and clearly described, and finally can gain first-hand an experiential sense of the responses produced. But the first two of these are denied us. In many ways the situation is analogous to that of the unfocused topics and holistic scoring used in the writing assessment. The difference is that the literature assessment took the final step and labeled student performance as "adequate" or "inadequate," something the writing assessment stopped short of doing. As was the case with Writing Report 10, persons may find Report 02-L-02, Responding to Literature the most useful source of information on the response exercises, for it includes a large number of the oral and written statements exactly as made.

To be sure, the response tasks were purposely kept unfocused, apparently because the assessors believed it would be useful to know how many responses from different ages would enter each of the Purves-Rippere categories. But is it? We must remember that the appearance of an engagement-involvement response, for example, does not substantiate the respondent's inability to make an interpretive or evaluative response. It merely indicates the kind of response one preferred to make initially on that particular occasion. Some teachers may consider this important knowledge to possess, but it is difficult to see why. Surely no one would claim that literature instruction should seek to alter students' initial-response preferences, though it may well aim to teach them *how* to make perception, interpretation, and evaluation responses when the need for these arises. But neither the channeling questions nor the essay topic measured ability to make any specific kind of response, only initial preference.

In general one feels that the response-to-literature exercises, despite the interest of researchers in this topic, provide very little in the way of significant and interpretable information, certainly less than one would expect given the amount of assessment time consumed. The point is important, since the exercises on understanding literary language were consequently quite limited in scope, in terms of both the range of literary concepts assessed and the representativeness of literary works included. Compared with the comprehensiveness of the reading assessment, that of literature seems meager. More could have been covered in the area of understanding literary language had less time been allocated to experimental response exercises.

Selecting the Content of a Literature Assessment

The issue of assessment content must be discussed from another point of view as well. Aside from the inclusion of the term "pun" and the names of literary genres used in the form-similarity exercises (fable, play, epic, essay, novel, letter, first-person narrative, biography, dialogue), the literature assessment omitted coverage of the terms and principles by means of which literary concepts are identified and spoken about. Had this occurred in mathematics or science, for example, the incredulous response of teachers would have been that NAEP had attempted to assess their area by ignoring its subject matter!

Presumably the assessors were stymied by the same problem that divides English teachers, a fundamental disagreement as to the nature of literature teaching, and therefore as to what an assessment of it should cover. As noted at the beginning of this chapter, everyone acknowledges that literature pleases and teaches about the human condition and that it does so notably and memorably by virtue of its esthetic properties. But here the agreement ends. To some the idea of teaching literature means using it instrumentally to help students learn about life vicariously and by examining their own. For others it means helping students learn how literature works in the doing of what it does, so that they will be able to read it more fully thereafter.

In caricatures familiar to all teachers, the former approach is seen as an endless bull session on anything and everything that merely glances off the surface of works being read. The latter appears as cold-blooded technical analysis and the naming of parts, or even worse, as the endless recitation of the facts and dates of literary history. In practice, of course, sensible literature teachers pursue elements of both approaches. But by failing to assess knowledge of literary terms and principles, NAEP in effect took sides on this basic issue and must now expect complaints from persons protesting the absurdity of a literature assessment that fails to cover what they believe to be the essential subject matter of literature teaching.

All things considered, the assessment content of greatest significance to teachers would seem to be the material on literary language, as well as the multiple-choice interpretation questions followed by written statements supporting one's choices. As discussed earlier, the importance of these exercises lies not in their numerical results, which are generally high for the older students, but rather in the extent to which they serve as models for classroom use. It cannot be overstressed that all literature teaching, apart from lecturing and answering student queries (and involving students in after-reading "projects" of various sorts), consists in the asking of assessment questions.

Most of the time, of course, the purpose of these questions is tutelary rather than testing or measurement, but in form they are assessment questions nonetheless. We ask them in order to engage students in considering parts and aspects of literary works that might otherwise escape their attention. In this way we teach our students how to read works of literature fully, just as students of music learn how to hear the full esthetic of a musical selection. The strengths and weaknesses of assessment exercises requiring focused engagement with literary works can become, and very likely already are, the strengths and weaknesses of our own classroom teaching. We owe a debt to National Assessment for highlighting this fact. Beyond this, there remains the problem of discovering meaningful ways of reporting the results of these and other questions when they are used for measurement or assessment. The NAEP performance on this score could stand considerable improvement.

Chapter Six

Summary Discussion

Results of the National Assessments of writing, reading, and literature have been presented and interpreted in detail. The principal thrust of the interpretive commentary pertaining to writing and reading was to stress the fact that many of our classroom teaching activities in these two subjects are assessments, formally speaking (although they are not tests), and thus may share in exactly the strengths and weaknesses noted in the National Assessment exercises. The main point of the reading assessment interpretation was to contrast assessment with commercial standardized achievement testing, to the end that we might more clearly recognize the limitations and abuses of such testing.

Beyond this, the following chapter makes no attempt to recapitulate assessment results. Rather it comments generally upon the level of learnings reflected in the three English assessments, presents the revised objectives slated for use in the second-round writing, reading, and literature assessments, summarizes positive aspects and problem areas of National Assessment, and advances a number of suggestions and cautions for use of National Assessment exercises and procedures at local levels.

Our Students' Knowledge of English

The correctness percentages reported for the hundreds of items of knowledge assessed at each age level represent baseline data against which the findings of subsequent assessment cycles will be compared. By themselves, however, the numbers have no meaning beyond the literal. That is, they indicate by extrapolation from the samples of respondents actually tested the percentages of young people throughout the country who possess a certain item of knowledge or are capable of performing a certain task. Beyond this, they are numbers standing in isolation.

Still, one asks, are the learning levels as high as they should be? For many, this remains the central question posed by the assessment

Summary Discussion

data. But the question has no answer. We must continually remember that assessment exercises were not selected for use because of the prior expectation that students at a certain age ought to be able to answer 70 or 80 percent of them correctly. This, of course, would be the standard procedure followed in classroom achievement testing. But the assessment was *not* a test of the amount of knowledge individual persons possess; it was and is a measure of how many persons at each age possess a given item of knowledge.

And naturally, items of varying degrees of difficulty were used. If not, if items had been selected that were equally difficult for each age, it would have appeared that everyone knows everything to the same degree of fullness. If the uniform difficulty level had been high, it would have seemed that no one knows anything; if low, that everyone knows everything perfectly. Furthermore, no item could have been used at more than one age. Cross-age comparisons would have been impossible, and the assessment would have told us nothing. In short, the difficulty of each exercise determined whether the correctness level would be high or low, and a mix of easy and difficult exercises was purposely used with each age group.

Readers are free, of course, to express whatever opinions they wish about the correctness percentages for individual exercises — that they seem high and thus indicate efficacious teaching and learning, or that they seem low and thus indicate the opposite. But no one advancing such opinions may claim special access to truth, and all must realize that the authority of their opinions derives solely from the validity of their prior assumptions about what young people at any age *ought* to know and be able to do. In other words, no one may point a finger at teacher incompetence or student ineptness just because, for example, "only" 30 percent of all thirteen year olds are capable of performing a certain task, unless and until one demonstrates in some convincing fashion that significantly more than 30 percent *ought* to possess this capability.

In several places in this booklet the author has expressed the opinion that individual totals seem surprisingly high or disturbingly low. Readers may accept or reject these opinions as they see fit. For what it is worth, however, members of the NCTE Committee to Study the National Assessment of Educational Progress agree that the assessment results, considered as a whole, are in no sense lower than they should be, however low that might be. This does not mean they are as high as possible, for no one knows what that would be either. It means only that there is no cause for alarm, and no evidence indicating that reading, language arts, and English teachers are not doing their jobs effectively, or that students are not learning what they ought to learn when they ought to learn it. Persons wishing to interpret assessment findings in a manner contrary to this, including in particular educational writers in the popular media, must assume responsibility for making explicit the basis of their interpretations.

Revised Objectives for the Second-Round Assessments

Since the release of objectives for the initial English language arts assessments, NAEP has commissioned additional numbers of teachers and scholars to revise the three sets of objectives and bring them into closer conformity with widely accepted professional desiderata. The revised objectives are as follows:

Writing

1. Demonstrate ability in writing to reveal personal feelings and ideas:
   a. through free expression;
   b. through the use of conventional modes of discourse.
2. Demonstrate ability to write in response to a wide range of societal demands and obligations (ability is defined to include correctness in usage, punctuation, spelling, and form or convention as appropriate to particular writing tasks, e.g., manuscripts, letters):
   a. social:
      1. personal,
      2. organizational,
      3. community;
   b. business/vocational;
   c. scholastic.
3. Indicate the importance attached to writing skills:
   a. recognize the necessity of writing for a variety of needs (as in 1 and 2);
   b. write to fulfill those needs;
   c. get satisfaction, even enjoyment, from having written something well.

Reading

1. Demonstrate behavior conducive to reading:
   a. demonstrate values related to reading:
      1. express an interest in reading,
      2. indicate an awareness of the value of reading,
      3. express a commitment to reading,
      4. read to fulfill personal needs;
   b. assess the readability of materials:
      1. determine readability of a particular selection,
      2. identify factors which affect readability;
   c. demonstrate knowledge of their own reading ability:
      1. identify material they can read and understand with ease,
      2. know the adequacy of their reading performance,
      3. know their own reading strengths and weaknesses.

Summary Discussion

2. Demonstrate word identification skills:
   a. know the letters of the alphabet;
   b. apply knowledge of sound symbol relationships;
   c. apply structural analysis techniques:
      1. use syllabication as an aid to pronunciation,
      2. identify the components of words;
   d. possess basic sight vocabulary;
   e. use context for word identification.
3. Possess skills for reading comprehension:
   a. utilize written language conventions as comprehension aids:
      1. understand the relationship of word order to meaning,
      2. use punctuation marks as an aid to understanding;
   b. demonstrate literal understanding of material read:
      1. identify the literal meaning of a word, phrase, or longer passage,
      2. recognize prefixes and suffixes as meaningful units,
      3. use function words as an aid to understanding;
   c. demonstrate inferential understanding of material read:
      1. derive implied meaning of a word, phrase, sentence or longer passage,
      2. use the connotation of a word as an aid to comprehension,
      3. use style or manner of expression as an aid to comprehension,
      4. understand the relationship of organization to meaning,
      5. identify the writer's intent,
      6. identify the underlying assumptions of the writer,
      7. make qualitative judgments about what is read,
      8. relate what is read to other reading,
      9. relate what is read to reality.
4. Use a variety of approaches in gathering information:
   a. demonstrate flexibility in adapting their rate of reading to suit their purpose(s) and the nature of the material:
      1. scan to locate specific information,
      2. skim for an overall impression,
      3. read for maximum comprehension;
   b. possess reading study skills:
      1. demonstrate efficient study techniques,
      2. use various parts of a book as study aids;
   c. use reference materials efficiently:
      1. demonstrate dictionary skills,
      2. demonstrate skills in using an encyclopedia,
      3. know other source materials and how to use them, e.g., card catalog, newspapers, directories, bibliography, abstracts, periodicals, indexes.

Literature

Assumptions. Literature is language used imaginatively. It communicates ideas and feelings. It expresses perceptions, interpretations, and visions of human experience. It exists in all cultures in all times, and it appears in oral, written, and enacted forms.

1. Experiences literature. Is aware that literary qualities exist in a variety of forms. Seeks experiences with literature in any form, from any culture:
   a. listens to literature:
      1. is aware of literary qualities in oral forms, such as poems, songs, jingles, jokes, nursery rhymes, story tellings, sermons, speeches, advertisements, and conversation,
      2. seeks to listen to oral forms of literature whether live or electronically reproduced;
   b. reads literature:
      1. is aware of literary qualities in written forms, such as letters, diaries, journals, essays, poems, autobiographies, biographies, histories, novels, short stories, plays, magazines, newspapers, catalogs, posters, advertisements, bumper stickers, tombstones, and graffiti,
      2. seeks to read written forms of literature;
   c. witnesses literature:
      1. is aware of literary qualities in enacted forms, such as plays, skits, operas, musicals, happenings, ceremonial and ritual activities, movies, and television productions,
      2. seeks to witness enacted forms of literature whether live or electronically reproduced.
2. Responds to literature—responds to literature in any form, from any culture, in a variety of ways—emotionally, reflectively, creatively—and shares responses with others:
   a. responds emotionally—participates emotionally in the world of a work of literature:
      1. experiences emotional involvement with characters and events in literature,
      2. experiences emotional involvement with the ideas and feelings expressed in literature,
      3. experiences emotional involvement with the language in a work of literature;
   b. responds reflectively—understands a work of literature by reflecting upon it in a variety of ways:
      1. understands a work of literature through its language and structure—comprehends the literal and figurative meanings of words and sentences in their contexts; comprehends the ways such elements as images, scenes, characters, and the

Summary Discussion

   ideas they embody work together to produce emotional effects and convey meanings;
   2. understands a work of literature through its relationship to the self—understands a work of literature and self by relating them to one another; relates kinds and patterns of experience in a work to personal experiences and values;
   3. understands a work of literature through its relationship to the world—understands a work by relating it to aspects of its own or other cultures; understands a work by relating it to other works of literature, other forms of art, and other modes of perceiving experience such as history, philosophy, psychology, sociology, anthropology, and theology;
   4. evaluates a work of literature—evaluates a work of literature by reflecting upon its language and structure, its relationship to the self, and its relationship to the world.
   c. responds creatively—uses language imaginatively in response to a work of literature:
   1. enacts a work of literature through oral and dramatic interpretation,
   2. recreates a work of literature through imitation or transformation in any form or medium,
   3. creates literature in any form or medium;
   d. shares responses with others—shares emotional, reflective, and creative responses in a variety of ways:
   1. communicates responses to others,
   2. participates with others in responding,
   3. shares works of literature with others.
3. Values literature—recognizes that literature plays a significant continuing role in the experience of the individual and society:
   a. recognizes that literature may be a source of enjoyment,
   b. recognizes that experience with literature may be a means of developing self-understanding and personal values,
   c. recognizes that experience with literature may be a means of understanding the nature of man and the diversity of culture,
   d. recognizes that literature may be a significant means of transmitting and sustaining the values of a culture.

Readers will see at once that the second-cycle objectives are considerably more elaborated than the original ones. Both the reading and the writing objectives are given with numerous examples of sample exercise content, illustrating the intention of each objective and how it might be assessed. Teachers and other educational personnel are encouraged to purchase copies of the revised objectives directly from National Assessment, since space limitations prohibit the inclusion of this important exemplifying content in the foregoing lists.

Notice that the reading objectives propose to deal separately with the various reading skills and should lead to the construction of exercises whose results will permit the various kinds of interpretations we were denied in the first reading assessment. Taken together, the new reading objectives constitute in skeletal fashion the skills component of a comprehensive K–12 instructional model in reading. School systems could well evaluate the scope of their own reading programs by reference to the second-cycle reading objectives.

The writing objectives now speak explicitly about correctness, but it is always correctness appropriate to particular writing tasks. Perhaps more importantly, personal writing and the free-form expression of feelings are now included, thus remedying what many teachers felt was a major oversight in the initial assessment. The three subcategories of social writing are also added. Topics included in exercises measuring objectives 1-b and 2 have been formulated with sufficient clarity to allow acceptable/unacceptable scoring from rubrics outlining the primary rhetorical trait(s) these topics elicit. The second-cycle writing objectives booklet contains sample topics together with exemplary student responses for each objective and should be of great interest to teachers of writing at every level.

The revised literature objectives broaden the notions of experiencing and responding to literature so that the former now includes listening and witnessing in addition to reading, while the latter embraces both emotional and intellectual responses, plus the sharing of these with others, as well as the possibility that a person's response to one work of literature may be the re-creation of that work in another form or medium, or even the creation of an entirely new work. Objective 3 seeks to measure cognitive grasp of the purpose and function of literature, things that most respondents in the first assessment were incapable of speaking about very clearly or coherently. Of the three, the new literature objectives may be the most difficult to translate into manageable exercises. But difficulty of measuring the effects of their teaching has never deterred literature teachers in the past, and it is unlikely to do so now. Whether National Assessment will be clever enough to handle the task imposed by the new objectives, only time will tell.

As of early 1975 the second-cycle writing assessment had been completed. The first results are tentatively slated for release in the first part of 1976, but budget cutbacks as of the moment dictate that most of the essay scoring will again be holistic, although the primary-trait rubrics may be made available to researchers in the field who wish to apply them to sample collections of the essays produced. Despite a reduction in its annual level of federal support from approximately six million dollars through 1973 to about four and a half million currently, NAEP has managed to keep the second reading assessment on its original schedule. Exercises are currently being administered and will continue into 1976, with results to appear perhaps by 1977. Timing of the second literature assessment is undecided, and NAEP is considering incorporating literature as one part of a new humanities assessment.

Positive Aspects of National Assessment

Readers will agree that National Assessment did a great many things sensibly, even creatively. Its overall model for the development of objectives and exercises, and the relating of the latter to the former, is exemplary. Commercial test manufacturers would be well-advised to borrow a leaf from NAEP methodology and publish sets of objectives in light of which their tests could be selected and evaluated by prospective users. Many classroom teachers, too, could afford to be more open with their students and communicate to them the nature of their teaching objectives.

All things considered, the NAEP exercises constitute a flexible consensus on what is worth measuring in the English language arts. The exercises utilized a variety of testing modes—oral, written, visual. They were task oriented and often, especially in writing and literature, called for actual student productions rather than merely the confirmation of a multiple-choice response written by the test maker. Their content was realistic, relevant, and wide-ranging, particularly in reading and somewhat less so in writing. On the whole, the NAEP exercises are grounds for a refreshing faith that a far greater range of competencies can be assessed than we earlier believed.

Classroom teachers should also find much of value in NAEP methodology. Surely it is important to define what is to be measured or tested and to ensure correspondence of measurement tasks with test objectives. It is important to utilize test exercises that are instructional in effect, as well as merely instruments for grading and labeling students. And it is important to employ a wide variety of exercise formats and content. Although neither was completely successful or free from criticism, the writing and the literature assessments did avoid a heavy emphasis on mechanics and terminology and thus constitute potentially healthy correctives to exaggerated classroom concern with these matters.

Perhaps the most important lesson for teachers, one stressed throughout this report, is that activities designed to assess are not limited to testing, but are featured throughout our teaching as well. The writing topics we use in our classes either are or are not sufficiently well defined, in point of the rhetorical tasks they require, to allow us to assess the writing they yielded in terms of the writer's ability to handle the task in question. If the topics are well defined, our assessment responses can be instructionally helpful in cases where the writer has failed to take up the task acceptably. If the topics are not well defined, our assessment responses must be limited either to mechanics at one extreme, or to overall quality at the other.

Similarly, we must remember that the questions we ask in teaching passages of reading and works of literature are assessment questions formally, even though we ask them for teaching purposes rather than for testing or measurement. In formulating these questions we must consider much the same things the NAEP assessors presumably had in mind in developing the reading and literature exercises, namely, aspects of content, organization, emphasis, logic, style, tone, and esthetic form that ought to be brought under the students' scrutiny in order that they may learn to read more fully and deeply on their own, whether they are reading literary texts or nonliterary ones. In general we should seek to incorporate the strengths of NAEP exercises on this score directly into our teaching, while at the same time avoiding their weaknesses and oversights.

Problem Areas: Motivational Level and Usefulness of the Data Collected

Despite the many positive aspects of National Assessment, there remain the inevitable problems. One is the assumption, already commented upon in the chapter on the writing assessment, that all respondents attended fully to the assessment questions and tried their best to answer them correctly. Attention, motivation, and effort are matters one usually takes for granted in discussing tests. Readers will recall, however, that the assessment items were administered by a specially trained professional staff who, though they were experienced in working with young people, were neither acquainted ahead of time with the students nor able to offer them the motivation of academic or other kinds of rewards, or even the promise of feedback on their individual performances. Almost certainly, therefore, the motivational climate of the assessment was less positive than one might have wished.

One may assume, of course, that low motivation affected all students more or less to the same extent and yielded scores proportionate across the board to what they would have been under optimal conditions. But we have no empirical evidence confirming this assumption, despite the relative ease of researching the question. One could simply administer a given set of assessment items to comparable samples of students under different motivational conditions. If motivational climate does affect all students equally, well and good. If not, if it turns out that the gap between boys and girls, for example, or between inner city and suburban students tends to be closed as motivation increases—not unreasonable expectations, given compulsiveness as a variable favoring upper social-class students, or docility as a variable affecting girls—then NAEP would be compelled to alter the conditions under which its exercises are administered. But the question *is* answerable, and researchers ought to set about answering it.

Another problem is that a fair amount of the data collected in the writing and literature assessments turned out to be of little use simply because no one understood how to analyze it meaningfully, other than to hold it for cross-time comparisons with data to be collected in subsequent assessments. One thinks immediately of the response-to-literature exercises and the holistically scored essay tasks. This is not to criticize National Assessment, which should be congratulated for its pioneering efforts to extend the range of valid measurement in English. Also, thanks to NAEP, rhetoricians have developed more precisely defined essay topics and the primary-trait scoring rubrics currently being used in the second-round writing assessment. When released, these should prove beneficial to writing teachers everywhere. Similarly, the assessors have contracted with a number of literature scholars for the development of improved assessment exercises in that area.

In a sense, then, what began as a problem turns out to be another plus factor for National Assessment. Not only has NAEP shown itself eager to remedy its initial defects and to do so by turning to subject-matter specialists rather than measurement experts, it has also done a service to English teaching generally by bringing to light areas of ignorance and faulty practice that prevail just as much in ordinary classrooms and local testing as they did in the initial assessments. And even if these problems aren't fully solved in second-round assessments, the way has been opened for additional study.

Problem Areas: Comprehensiveness of the Assessments

Still another problem concerns the comprehensiveness of exercise content in the several assessments. As noted from the outset, the exercises actually used in any one assessment constitute only a sample of those required to exhaustively measure attainment of assessment objectives, which are global in scope. No claims for comprehensive representativeness of the exercise samples can be made. In fact, there is no way to decide the question of comprehensiveness except by reference to particular instructional models designed by individual schools or teachers to implement given sets of objectives.

Though jargony, the phrase "instructional model" refers merely to a set of specific statements telling exactly what material is to be taught to whom, when, and to what degree of mastery. These statements fill in the gap, so to speak, between general sets of objectives like those used in the assessments and exercise batteries designed to comprehensively measure attainment of just those skills and knowledge a given teacher or school is teaching.

NAEP could not assume even the most basic instructional model as a common denominator nationally because the actualities of teaching differ widely from locale to locale, building to building, and classroom to classroom. Instead it had to formulate objectives sufficiently general in their wording to be acceptable nationwide, then measure the attainment of these objectives by use of groups of exercises loosely keyed to each general objective, without recourse to the intervening specifics of an instructional model. These facts do not vitiate the inferences one may draw about the general state of knowledge nationally or in the assessment subgroups. But limitations would definitely show up if NAEP exercises were used verbatim at the local level, either as mastery tests or as measures of teacher effectiveness.

A Warning against the Local Use of NAEP Exercises

In light of the foregoing, a warning should be issued against the use of NAEP exercises locally, whether throughout a district or system or within a single building. As is discussed quite fully below, it is highly desirable to utilize NAEP procedures in manufacturing and administering one's own exercises fitting the local instructional model. But it is quite a different thing to use the NAEP exercises themselves. Unfortunately, however, the latter is becoming the rule, owing to the availability of National Assessment exercises and the unexamined assumption that if they are valid nationally, they must be acceptable locally.

Use of NAEP exercises within individual school districts or buildings is a form of Russian roulette. Let us suppose, for example, that the NAEP writing items are administered to eighth graders in a certain building. Miss Brown's class happen recently to have written letters to a city official inviting him to judge a class contest, let us say, and also have role-played on toy telephones and practiced recording their mock conversations. (See exercises 4 and 9 in Table 1 of this booklet.) Mr. Smith's class have just completed units on sensory description and the writing of cinquaines and haiku. Other things being equal, Brown's students will probably outperform high school seniors nationally, while Smith's will be fortunate to equal the eighth-grade average.

To regard such results as valid indices of student achievement and/or teacher competence would be a travesty. These qualities must be measured exclusively in terms of the instructional model actually used in the classroom, building, or district in question. National Assessment exercises are wrong for the purpose, just as commercial achievement tests are also wrong.

Limitations of Statewide Uses of NAEP Exercises

It is natural to expect that entire states might wish to conduct an assessment using NAEP exercises so that they could compare the level of knowledge of their students with national and regional totals. Here too, problems await the unwary. Suppose the education officials of a certain state enlist the aid of an NAEP sampling expert, who arranges a state sample having the same subgroup composition as that used nationally. But instead of hiring special test administrators at great cost, the state officials send the exercise packets into the field with written instructions for administration by regular teachers.

No matter how rigidly the teachers adhere to the instructions, the simple fact that the exercises are presented by the students' own teachers is almost certain to guarantee higher motivation and effort on their part, enough perhaps that average correctness levels may exceed by five or ten percentage points what would have been attained under NAEP's test conditions. No one knows for sure, but the chances are excellent that the difference would be enough to make the state in question appear to outperform the total NAEP sample from its region.

At this writing, at least fourteen states have utilized all or a portion of the NAEP reading exercises in state assessments. But even if statewide assessments are administered by specially-trained professionals under conditions identical to those used by NAEP, what can these states hope to learn? Louisiana, for example, compared median correctness levels for all exercises achieved by its students with the medians achieved by the Southeast region in the nationwide assessment. Louisiana nine year olds were five percentage points below the Southeast, the thirteens were two percentage points below, and the seventeens five points above. The law of averages (and medians) dictates that some must be above the central measure and some below it. This is precisely what Louisiana found—above in one age group and below in two others.

Furthermore, the differences are trivial, rather on the order of worrying about whether your neighbor's net worth is a thousand dollars greater or less than yours, instead of whether he is wealthy and you are on the dole. More importantly, there is simply no reason to believe that a sample of 2000 young people at a given age in any state in the nation, if stratified in a way proportionate to the NAEP subgroups, will differ by any meaningful amount from the national level. The key issue, of course, is the definition of "meaningful." In the author's opinion, differences of five people per hundred one way or another are simply not worth worrying about. States would do far better to stop wasting funds comparing themselves with national and regional levels from which they do not differ to any significant magnitude and to spend the money instead dealing with pockets of known educational deprivation.

Local Accountability Measurement Using NAEP Procedures

Although the National Assessment exercises themselves are unsuited for local use, NAEP's procedures, properly understood and applied, are of great potential value in designing programs to measure the achievement, popularly termed "accountability," of given educational units—individual classes, the classes of individual teachers, entire buildings, or complete school districts. Understanding the rationale involved, however, requires a fundamental reorientation of our typical view of measuring academic success. The point is important and will be dwelt upon at some length.

To see how NAEP methodology provides an enlightened approach to the thorny question of accountability, let us step back from schooling momentarily and think about the two ways in which the world judges success and excellence generally. We might term one of these a rank-ordered "winners-and-losers" model, and the other a non-ranked "performance-criterion" model. Consider athletics, where the winners-and-losers model prevails. If five sprinters are running a hundred-yard dash, we expect to see one winner and four losers. In fact, though, the top accolade could just as easily be awarded to each and every runner who finishes under a criterion time of ten seconds, for example, just as every child at summer camp able to swim a mile receives the same ribbon regardless of whose time is fastest.

In working for wages, however, the performance-criterion model ordinarily holds sway. Assembly-line workers who complete one unit every eight minutes, for example, are assured of their jobs and have nothing but idle time to gain by working faster. The thrust towards equal-work rules pursued from the outset by the American labor movement represents in effect a rejection of the winners-and-losers model, where a man or woman could be assured of a job only by continually trying to work harder and faster than the others, in favor of a performance-criterion model, where every man or woman knows what the work must be and that meeting that standard will guarantee success.

Returning to schools, we note that academic evaluation is almost always conducted on the winners-and-losers model, by virtue of the procedures we use to rank-order students relative to one another, awarding those at the top (the winners) grades of A, and so on down the ranking. Although more and more teachers in recent years have shifted to performance-criterion grading ("There's an A for anyone who can earn it. Here are the criteria you must meet . . ."), most of us continue to assign grades by rank-ordering students and evaluating their performance according to their group standing, giving A's to those on top, and failures to those on the bottom.

But notice what happens when this winners-and-losers model is suggested for use in evaluating the achievement of teachers. Suppose a school board decides it will give special-merit salary increases to the top third of its teachers at each grade level and proposes to determine this top third by rank-ordering the average performance of each teacher's classes on a standardized reading test. In other words, the one-third group of teachers whose classes have the highest average percentile or grade-level scores at year's end (or gains scores, for that matter) will get the extra money, while the lower two thirds get nothing.

Naturally the teachers would scream bloody murder at such a proposal, and well they should. For no matter how successful all might be in absolute terms in raising their students' reading scores, only one third can be above two thirds in a rank-ordering, and it is thus foreordained that only one teacher in three can qualify for the salary increase. Presumably the teachers would immediately counter their school board's offer with the proposal that *any* teacher whose students average above a certain preestablished score should qualify for the merit increase, thereby signaling their rejection of winners and losers in favor of a performance criterion, perhaps one which they themselves would have a say in establishing.

The pernicious logic of rank-ordered evaluation is that "getting better" has meaning only in terms of getting better *than someone else*. This is equally true whether we are speaking of the academic achievement of students or the teaching success of teachers. People rise only by virtue of pushing others down, relatively speaking. There can be no thought of succeeding or failing on one's own in the attainment of a given standard of achievement, only the ennervating sense of happening to have been better or poorer than those with whom we are compared. As teachers, we rightfully resist having our teaching competence thus called to account, although we routinely evaluate the work of students in this fashion. And of course, standardized achievement tests and college entrance examinations are the quintessential rank-ordering instruments.

All of which brings us around to the alternative of using NAEP methodology to measure the achievement of local educational units on a performance-criterion rather than a winners-and-losers basis. In such a case, the educational units would not be rank-ordered in mutual comparison. Rather, they would be categorized according to whether each meets or fails to meet the criteria of achievement deemed appropriate to its particular situation.

The main ideas to remember are two in number. First, the National Assessment approach gauges levels of learning by asking how many students know an individual item of knowledge rather than by asking (as achievement tests do) how many items of knowledge are known by each individual student. Second, any educational unit being evaluated can employ test exercises tailored expressly to its own instructional model and, more importantly, can have a say in determining for each exercise the correctness percentage that will stand as the criterion of successful teaching and learning.

The process might work as follows. Suppose a medium-sized city wished to evaluate the effectiveness of reading instruction by the end of grade six throughout all of its elementary buildings. Committees of teachers in each building, using NAEP exercises as models, would develop a modest battery of reading exercises (perhaps the equivalent of one hour of testing per student, three hours total using different samples of students) consonant with the instructional model existing in that school. Or the exercises might be selected on a similar basis from among a master set provided by the central administrative office.

For each exercise so constructed or selected, the committee of teachers would recommend a correctness percentage to stand as the performance criterion applicable to their building. If 65 percent were decided upon (in the case of a medium-difficulty exercise, for example) this would mean that the teaching in that building would be accounted successful if 65 percent or more of the sample of students answering the exercise got it correct. Another building might have a 70 percent correctness criterion set for its students on the same or a similar exercise, and still another only 55 percent. Decisions about what criteria to stipulate would be made with reference to a wide range of data applicable to each building individually. The process of deciding criteria would in all likelihood be participated in by central administrators and outside consultants as well as by the teachers and administrators of the building in question.

The goal of all parties would be to settle upon the fairest possible success criterion in each individual case. To be adjudged successful overall, buildings would have to meet or exceed their success criteria, let us say, on four out of five (80 percent) of the exercises in their test batteries. All buildings that achieved the 80 percent overall success level would be considered top schools without difference or distinction, and the opportunity to achieve this standing would be open to every building. Those that failed to do so would of course receive additional support and attention.

Advantages of NAEP-Style Accountability Measurement

Consider the many important advantages of the procedure just outlined for local assessments of accountability.
1. Test exercises would be constructed or selected by the teachers whose teaching achievements are being measured, in accordance with what they know their students have been taught.
2. Exercise content would reflect the instructional model and other conditions actually present in individual classes, buildings, or districts.

3. Teachers would have a say in stipulating the correctness percentages that would serve as success criteria for the exercises used in their classes or buildings.
4. Success criteria would be decided in light of the learning potential of the children, their prior learning attainments, relative degree of socioeconomic disadvantagement, cultural background, and so on.
5. Because of the sampling procedures used, no one exercise would be answered by all students, and some students would not need to be tested at all in a given assessment. As a result, there would be no way to rank-order student performances as standardized achievement tests do now, and thus no way to continually stigmatize those students who by accident of birth are less intelligent and/or socioeconomically advantaged than their age-mates, and who therefore perpetually find themselves at the lower end of these rank-orderings.
6. Commercial standardized achievement tests would no longer be administered, and percentile rankings and grade-level scores would become relics of an outmoded educational era.
7. Individual students would naturally continue to be graded according to their academic achievement in class, but the grading would be done by the persons best able to do it justly—their individual classroom teachers.
8. Perhaps most important to teachers and building administrators, the personnel of any educational unit evaluated in this manner would know ahead of time exactly how well their students would have to perform if their teaching were to be accounted successful. Furthermore, success could be attained by any and all of these educational units. Failure would be possible, of course, but it would come as a result of not measuring up to one's own standard, and never from accident of falling at the lower end of a relativistic rank-ordering.

Final Thoughts on Measuring Teaching and Learning

The NAEP-style accountability procedures just proposed would in no way diminish competition among students or the general pursuit of excellence in both teaching and learning. And to be sure, there are times when deciding winners and losers is wholly appropriate. Nearly everyone, for example, enjoys a good boxing match between evenly matched prizefighters. Similarly, the holistic scoring of inter-mixed matched samples of essays written at different points in time, as discussed earlier in Chapter Three, is a perfectly valid way of determining differences in overall quality between the two samples. But who would take pleasure in seeing a featherweight forced into the ring with Muhammad Ali? And who would want to make a judgment about the general quality of writing produced at different times if it had to be based on a comparison of only the best essays from Time A with just the poorest from Time B? Playing "winners and losers" in these instances would be absurdly unjust.

Yet this is precisely what we do in education when we administer standardized achievement tests yielding rank-ordered results to students who are being taught different content by different methods in different buildings and localities and who come to school from widely diverse home conditions and varying socioeconomic levels and culturally pluralistic value systems. Our present methods of conducting widescale evaluation of academic achievement are fine for those who enjoy a Christians-vs-lions type of competition, but are hardly worthy of the era of social enlightenment in which we claim to be living.

Furthermore, as teachers our recognition of the injustice of standardized methods of assessing student achievement becomes starkly apparent, as was noted above, each time a school-board member suggests an accountability scheme for assessing teachers' competence on the basis of their students' achievement-test scores. We *know* these achievement tests are unfair to us as teachers. What we are less able or less willing to recognize is that they are just as unfair to students.

Why then do our schools continue to use these standardized test instruments? As educators we pride ourselves justifiably in our ability to decide what should be taught, yet we shrink from the responsibility of measuring the effectiveness of our teaching in its own terms, placing our confidence instead in tests designed by persons totally unacquainted with our work. Collectively we are haunted by the fear of coming out second best in comparisons set up by someone else. Thus we seek a perverse security in commercial achievement tests not of our making nor of teachers anywhere.

Laymen are no different. Whether parents of schoolchildren or board members voting on school budgets, the question they ask is seldom whether their schools are achieving self-set learning objectives, but rather how well the local students compare with those in the next town over, or how they stand on commercial achievement tests comparing them with the country at large.

Americans in general seem unable to trust their local educational professionals to evaluate the achievement of their young people. Nor do we as teachers seem secure in making this judgment on our own. It is as if a patient were to ask his doctor not whether he is sick or well, but whether he is sicker or weller than the other persons in town, and as if the doctor in turn were to refuse judgment until he had examined the other people and rank-ordered his findings.

Obviously, an excellent way for schools to change all this would be to switch over to the use of locally determined assessment exercises and performance criteria as suggested above. This arrangement should satisfy everyone's concerns about the learning levels of students generally, and about the effectiveness of local educational units, whether individual teachers, grade levels, or entire buildings. It would be a fair means of measuring accountability, in that failure is foreordained for no one. In the author's view, an educator would be rightly judged irresponsible who shrank from having his or her professional competence so assessed.

Standardized achievement tests would soon pass out of existence as we grew accustomed to relying upon National Assessment for all the regional and nationwide measurement needed in order to establish a background context of normal educational levels. As longitudinal (across time) data accrue from subsequent assessment rounds, we could chart uptrends and downtrends in student achievement and would remain on the alert for local manifestations of these.

Commercial test makers might be forced to close their doors for want of business, although the enterprising among their number, like turn-of-the-century grain and harness merchants who went into the gasoline business, might very well begin to manufacture pools of assessment exercises to be purchased on a per-item basis by local educational units. The selection of exercises and the setting of performance criteria would be handled locally, while the manufacture of test booklets containing the items selected and/or developed by the teachers, plus the scoring, could be performed by the commercial testing corporations.

In the end, once we have learned how to assess the achievement of students and teachers in the manner here proposed, without reliance upon the manifestly unjust rank-order logic of standardized achievement tests, we shall be able to turn our attention to the *real* questions spotlighted by National Assessment and certain to reappear in every local assessment—How are schools to cope with and compensate for the learning deficits of students who are economically deprived, students who live in inner cities, students whose parents have little education, and students who possess the foregoing characteristics and also happen to be black or members of other disadvantaged minorities? And to a far lesser extent, students who live in the Southeast, and students who happen to be males?

Statistical geneticists to the contrary, nothing in nature requires that these young people should lag behind their more fortunate peers. Yet the National Assessment data clearly indicates that they do, and as teachers we know from everyday experience that they do. Thus it is the great challenge to the educational profession to attempt to compensate through in-school nurture for what these children have lacked of it on the outside thus far in their lives.

The National Assessment of Educational Progress cannot tell us how to accomplish this task. But it *can* serve as a constant reminder of how badly these students need our help and how wrong we are to continue measuring their achievement at local levels by forcing them into rank-order comparisons with their more favored brothers and sisters. And the subgroup results to be reported in future assessment rounds *can* tell us whether our compensatory programs on their behalf are working or not by providing collective evidence of gap-closing between, for example, males and females, blacks and non-blacks, inner cities and wealthy suburbs, the Southeast and the Northeast, and so on.

All our instincts towards compassion and social justice, not to mention research findings on how to optimize learning environments, cry out for a change in our methods of evaluating the educational achievement of disadvantaged youth. Assessments conducted regularly at the nationwide level under the aegis of National Assessment, plus local assessments utilizing NAEP procedures coupled with individualized performance criteria, offer a valid and responsible alternative to current practice, an alternative that merits our most urgent attention. By thus removing the "measurement monkey" from our backs without in any sense shrinking from the responsibility to give a good accounting of our professional performance, we can open the way to a bright new day in the teaching of English and the language arts.

Appendix A

Reading Passages

Following are verbatim transcripts of eleven of the passages used in the reading assessment. These passages are included because the questions asked about them require the drawing of inferences or the generalizing of main idea or organizational structure and can be evaluated only in context of the entire passage.

A Stormy Day

The wind pushed the boat farther and farther out to sea. It started to rain and the fog grew thick. The boy and his father were lost at sea.

Beat Generation

Any attempt to label an entire generation is unrewarding, and yet the generation which went through the last war, or at least could get a drink easily once it was over, seems to possess a uniform, general quality which demands an adjective. It was John Kerouac, the author of a fine, neglected novel "The Town and the City," who finally came up with it. It was several years ago, when the face was harder to recognize, but he had a sharp, sympathetic eye, and one day he said, "You know, this is really a *beat* generation." The origins of the word "beat" are obscure, but the meaning is only too clear to most Americans. More than mere weariness, it implies the feeling of having been used, of being raw. It involves a sort of nakedness of mind, and, ultimately, of soul; a feeling of being reduced to the bedrock of consciousness. In short, it means being undramatically pushed up against the wall of oneself. A man is beat whenever he goes for broke and wagers the sum of his resources on a single number; and the young generation has done that continually from early youth. (From "This Is the Beat Generation," Elellan Holmes. *The Character of Prose*, New York Times Company.)

Easter Eggs

Almost seven hundred years ago, King Edward of England bought 450 Easter eggs painted gold and other bright colors. He paid about

18 cents for all of them. Prices have gone way up since then. Easter eggs have been made not only from real eggs. Some of the most beautiful were fancy oval-shaped objects of silver and enamel, colorful stones or glass. Many had ribbons, beads, or feathers on them. Some of the tastiest looking eggs could not be fried or boiled. They were made of chocolate or of sugar-filled candy. During the 19th century, candy eggs with a window at one end and tiny scenes inside were given as gifts. In England messages and dates were written on the eggs, and in Scotland children were given hard-boiled eggs as toys on Easter Sunday.

Farmer Brown

One spring Farmer Brown had an unusually good field of wheat. Whenever he saw any birds in this field, he got his gun and shot as many of them as he could. In the middle of the summer he found that his wheat was being ruined by insects. With no birds to feed on them, the insects had multiplied very fast. What Farmer Brown did not understand was this: A bird is not simply an animal that eats food the farmer may want for himself. Instead, it is one of many links in the complex surroundings, or *environment*, in which we live.

How much grain a farmer can raise on an acre of ground depends on many factors. All of these factors can be divided into two big groups. Such things as the richness of the soil, the amount of rainfall, the amount of sunlight, and the temperature belong together in one of these groups. This group may be called *non-living factors*. The second group may be called *living factors*. The living factors in any plant's environment are animals and other plants. Wheat, for example, may be damaged by wheat rust, a tiny plant that feeds on wheat; or it may be eaten by plant-eating animals such as birds or grasshoppers....

It is easy to see that the relations of plants and animals to their environment are very complex, and that any change in the environment is likely to bring about a whole series of changes. (From Bertha Morris Parker, *Balance in Nature*. Harper and Row, Publishers.)

Frangibles

After two weeks of unusually high-speed travel we reached Xeno, a small planet whose population, though never before visited by Earthmen, was listed as "friendly" in the *Interstellar Gazetteer*.

On stepping lightly (after all, the gravity of Xeno is scarcely more than twice that of our own moon) from our spacecraft we saw that "friendly" was an understatement. We were immediately surrounded by Frangibles of various colors, mostly pinkish or orange, who held out their "hands" to us. Imagine our surprise when their "hands" actually merged with ours as we tried to shake them!

Then, before we could stop them (how could we have stopped them?), two particularly pink Frangibles simply stepped right into two eminent scientists among our party, who immediately lit up with the same pink glow. While occupied in this way, the scientists reported afterwards, they suddenly discovered they "knew" a great deal about Frangibles and life on Xeno.

Apparently Frangibles could take themselves apart atomically and enter right into any other substance. They communicated by thought waves, occasionally merging "heads" for greater clarity. Two Frangibles who were in love with each other would spend most of their time merged into one; they were a bluish-green color unless they were having a lover's quarrel, when they turned gray. (From Martha S. Clapp, *Space Trip*. Copyright 1966 by Martha S. Clapp.)

Helen Keller

Helen Keller was born in 1880 in Tuscumbia, Alabama. When she was two years old, she lost her sight and hearing as the result of an illness. In 1886 she became the pupil of Anne Sullivan, who taught Helen to "see" with her fingertips, to "hear" with her feet and hands, and to communicate with other people. Miss Sullivan succeeded in arousing Helen's curiosity and interest by spelling the names of objects into her hand. At the end of three years Helen had mastered both the manual and the braille alphabet and could read and write. She began speech lessons in 1890 with Sarah Fuller. Helen entered Radcliffe College in 1900 and was elected vice-president of her freshman class. She completed her studies and was graduated with honors in 1904. After graduation, Helen began to study the problems of the blind. She toured the United States, Europe and Asia, giving lectures on behalf of the handicapped. She also wrote many books and articles, including an autobiography of her early years. (From the *Golden Home and High School Encyclopedia*, Volume 10. Western Publishing Company.)

Skiing

Skiing has recently become one of the more popular sports in the United States. Because of its popularity, thousands of winter vacationers are flying north rather than south. In many areas, reservations are required months ahead of time.

I discovered the accommodation shortage through an unfortunate experience. On a sunny Saturday morning I set out from Denver for the beckoning slopes of Aspen, Colorado. After passing signs for other ski areas, I finally reached my destination. Naturally I lost no time in heading for the nearest tow. After a stimulating afternoon of miscalculated stem turns I was famished. Well, one thing led to another and it must have been eight o'clock before I concerned myself with a bed for my bruised and aching bones.

It took precisely one phone call to ascertain the lack of lodgings in the Aspen area. I had but one recourse. My auto and I started the treacherous jaunt over the pass and back toward Denver. Along the way, I went begging for a bed. Finally a jolly tavern-keeper took pity and for only thirty dollars a night allowed me the privilege of staying in a musty, dirty bathless room above his tavern.

Sports Cars

A sports car differs from an ordinary passenger car in that its size and number of accessories are limited. The sports car also differs from the ordinary passenger car in performance. It can attain higher speeds because it is built smaller and lower. For these reasons it can also turn corners faster and more smoothly than a passenger car. Also a sports car generally gets better gas mileage than an ordinary passenger car. (From the *Golden Home and High School Encyclopedia*, Volume 7. Western Publishing Company.)

Suburbanites

Suburbanites are not irresponsible. Indeed, what is striking about the young couples' march along the abyss is the earnestness and precision with which they go about it. They are extremely budget-conscious. They can rattle off most of their monthly payments down to the last penny; one might say that even their impulse buying is deliberately planned. They are conscientious in meeting obligations, and rarely do they fall delinquent in their accounts.

They are exponents of what could be called *budgetism*. This does not mean that they actually keep formal budgets—quite the contrary. The beauty of budgetism is that one doesn't have to keep a budget at all. It's done automatically. In the new middle-class rhythm of life, obligations are homogenized, for the overriding aim is to have oneself precommitted to regular monthly payments on all the major items.

Americans used to be divided into three sizable groups: those who thought of money obligations in terms of the week, of the month, and of the year. Many people remain at both ends of the scale, but with the widening of the middle class, the mortgage payments are firmly geared to a thirty-day cycle, and any dissonant peaks and valleys are anathema. Just as young couples are now paying winter fuel bills in equal monthly fractions through the year, so they seek to spread out all the other heavy seasonal obligations they can anticipate. If vendors will not oblige by accepting equal monthly installments, the purchasers will smooth out the load themselves by floating loans.

It is, suburbanites cheerfully explain, a matter of psychology. They don't trust themselves. In self-entrapment is security. They try to budget so tightly that there are no unappropriated funds, for they know these would burn a hole in their pocket. Not merely out of greed for goods, then, do they commit themselves; it is protection they want, too. And though it would be extreme to say that they go into debt to be secure, carefully charted debt does give them a certain peace of mind—and in suburbia this is more coveted than luxury itself. (From William H. Whyte, *The Organization Man*. Doubleday & Company, Inc.)

Turtle Poem

My body a rounded stone
with a pattern of smooth seams,
My head a short snake,
retractive, projective.
My legs come out of their sleeves
or shrink within,
and so does my chin.
My eyelids are quick clamps.

My back is my roof.
I am always at home.
I travel where my house walks.
It is a smooth stone.
It floats within the lake,
or rests in the dust.
My flesh lives tenderly
Inside its home.

(From May Swenson, *To Mix with Time*. Charles Scribner's Sons.)

Village of Nayon

Until about thirty years ago, the village of Nayon seems to have been a self-sufficient agricultural community with a mixture of native and sixteenth century Spanish customs. Lands were abandoned when too badly eroded. The balance between population and resources allowed a minimum subsistence. A few traders exchanged goods between Quito and the villages in the tropical barrancas, all within a radius of ten miles. Houses had dirt floors, thatched roofs, and pole walls that were sometimes plastered with mud. Guinea pigs ran freely about each house and were the main meat source. Most of the population spoke no Spanish. Men wore long hair and concerned themselves chiefly with farming.

The completion of the Guayaquil-Quito railway in 1908 brought the first real contacts with industrial civilization to the high inter-Andean valley. From this event gradually flowed not only technological changes, but new ideas and social institutions. Feudal social relationships no longer seemed right and immutable; medicine and public health improved; elementary education became more common; urban

Quito began to expand; and finally—and perhaps least important so far—modern industries began to appear, although even now on a most modest scale.

In 1948–49, the date of our visit, only two men wore their hair long; and only two old-style houses remained. If guinea pigs were kept, they were penned; their flesh was now a luxury food, and beef the most common meat. Houses were of adobe or fired brick, usually with tile roofs, and often contained five or six rooms, some of which had plank or brick floors. Most of the population spoke Spanish. There was no resident priest, but an appointed government official and a policeman represented authority. A six-teacher school provided education. Clothing was becoming citified; for men it often included overalls for work and a tailored suit, white shirt, necktie, and felt hat for trips to Quito. Attendance at church was low and many festivals had been abandoned. Volleyball or soccer was played weekly in the plaza by young men who sometimes wore shorts, blazers and berets. There were few shops, for most purchases were made in Quito, and from there came most of the food, so that there was a far more varied diet than twenty-five years ago. There were piped water and sporadic health services; in addition, most families patronized Quito doctors in emergencies.

The crops and their uses had undergone change. Maize, or Indian corn, was still the primary crop, but very little was harvested as grain. Almost all was sold in Quito as green corn to eat boiled on the cob, and a considerable amount of the corn eaten as grain in Nayon was imported. Beans, which do poorly here, were grown on a small scale for household consumption. Though some squash was eaten, most was exported. Sweet potatoes, tomatoes, cabbage, onions, peppers and at lower elevations, sweet yucca and arrowroot were grown extensively for export; indeed, so export-minded was the community that it was almost impossible to buy locally grown produce in the village. People couldn't be bothered with retail sales. (From "The Village in an Industrial World," *Scientific Monthly*, August 1953.)

Whistling Wind

The wind whistled woefully as it wound its way through the nearly leafless trees. The pale yellow moon cast eerie shadows as it slipped in and out from behind the clouds like a blinking flashlight. Strange figures could be seen dashing and darting through the streets. Ghosts, goblins—what could they be? What do they want? Whom have they come to haunt? Beware . . .

Appendix B

Literary Works

Following are the six poems used in connection with the personal response items in the literature assessment. The three short stories used are cited by publisher's reference only.

Poem

As the cat
climbed over
the top of

the jamcloset
first the right
forefoot

carefully
then the hind
stepped down

into the pit of
the empty
flowerpot

— William Carlos Williams

The Closing of the Rodeo

The lariat snaps; the cowboy rolls
His pack, and mounts and rides away.
Back to the land the cowboy goes.

Plumes of smoke from the factory sway
in the setting sun. The curtain falls,
A train in the darkness pulls away.

Goodbye, says the rain on the iron roofs.
Goodbye, say the barber poles.
Dark drum the vanishing horses' hooves.

— William Jay Smith

Sport

Hunters, hunters
Follow the chase
I saw the Fox's eyes,
Not in his face
But on it, big with fright
Haste, hunters, haste!

Say, hunters, say
Is it a noble sport?
As rats that bite
Babies in cradles, so
Such rats and men
Take their delight.

—W. H. Davies

If apples were pears,
And peaches were plums
And the rose had a different name;
If tigers were bears,
And fingers were thumbs,
I'd love you just the same!

—Anonymous

Space Travellers

There was a witch, hump-backed and hooded,
   Lived by herself in a burnt-out tree.
When storm winds shrieked and the moon was buried
   And the dark of the forest was black as black,
     She rose in the air like a rocket at sea,
        Riding the wind,
        Riding the night,
     Riding the tempest to the moon and back.

There may be a man with a hump of silver,
   Telescope eyes and a telephone ear,
Dials to twist and knobs to twiddle,
   Waiting for a night when skies are clear,
     To shoot from the scaffold with a blazing track,
        Riding the dark,
        Riding the cold,
     Riding the silence to the moon and back.

—James N. Britton

Into My Heart an Air That Kills

Into my heart an air that kills
From yon far country blows:
What are those blue remembered hills,
What spires, what farms are those?

That is the land of lost content,
I see it shining plain,
The happy highways where I went
And cannot come again.
—A. E. Housman

Short Stories

"Sam, Bangs and Moonshine," by Evaline Ness. Holt, Rinehart and Winston.
"Half a Gift," by Robert Zacks. MacIntosh and Otis.
"Snake Dance," by Corey Ford. Liberty Publications.